EUREKA!

RICHARD PLATT

EUREKA!

Great Inventions
and how they Happened

RICHARD PLATT

KINGFISHER

BOSTON

FOREWORD

SIR PAUL NURSE

"If you took away everything in the world that had to be invented, there'd be nothing left except a lot of people getting rained on."
Tom Stoppard

We are living in a time of unprecedented discovery and invention. Scientists have now sequenced the entire human genome; animals, from sheep to cats, have been cloned; the Internet is changing the way we work, teach, and run our businesses; and major advances in biology, chemistry, and physics are transforming medicine. New technology—including super conductors, quantum computers, and nanotechnology—will provide the tools for the next leap forward in scientific progress and a continuation of human achievement that dates back to before Galileo's invention of the pendulum in 1581.

All of the discoveries and inventions detailed in **Eureka!**—starting with the pendulum—have one thing in common: individuals who, in the words of the scientist Albert Szent-Györgyi, were able to see what everybody else had seen but think what nobody else had thought.

A few discoveries came out of accidents—antibiotics being probably the most famous—but behind some others lie many years of investigation and hard work. My own discovery of a gene that sheds light on our understanding of how all living things grow and reproduce—and how cancer cells go wrong—exemplifies the typical discovery process: a great deal of thought, a great deal of work, plenty of failure, and if you're lucky, eureka! It hits you, and you realize that you have solved the problem.

The "eureka moment" is incredibly exciting but incredibly short—often a source of frustration in the laboratories where I work. The discovery itself may not always be something that will make a huge impact on society, and it can often take many years before its importance is realized. In my own field—the biology of cancer—most of the advances that are published each month are incremental, but over time they help build a picture of a system or a process that ultimately points the way to greater advances.

The discoveries presented in **Eureka!** highlight where a curious and inquiring mind can lead and illustrate why science is so important today. Without eureka moments we cannot improve the world we live in. But scientific discoveries are not made in isolation from society. The consequences of a discovery may have major moral or ethical implications. For example, new medical genetics will provide doctors with the tools and information to help prevent or treat certain diseases, but without safety measures that information could be misused and lead to discrimination.

In order to shape and influence how new tools and technology are used and to ensure appropriate safety measures are in place, it is important to have a good understanding of the underlying science, and there is no better place to start than at the eureka moment—the moment of discovery.

Paul Nurse

Sir Paul Nurse, Joint Director-General of Cancer Research U.K.

To my inventive niece Bethan

Publishing Manager: Melissa Fairley
Designer: Mark Bristow
Picture Researcher: Rachael Swann
Production Controller: Nancy Roberts
DTP Coordinator: Sarah Pfitzner
Artwork Archivists: Wendy Allison, Jenny Lord
Proofreaders: Sheila Clewley, Sue Lightfoot
Coordinating Editor: Sarah Snavely
Indexer: Sue Lightfoot

KINGFISHER
a Houghton Mifflin Company imprint
222 Berkeley Street
Boston, Massachusetts 02116
www.houghtonmifflinbooks.com

First published in 2003
2 4 6 8 10 9 7 5 3 1
1TR/0703/TIMES/PICA(PICA)/150MA

LIBRARY OF CONGRESS CATALOGING-IN-PUBLICATION DATA
Platt, Richard.
Eureka! / by Richard Platt; foreword by Paul Nurse.
p. cm
1. Inventions—History—Juvenile literature.
2. Inventors—History—Juvenile literature.
I. Title.
T15.P623 2003
609—dc21

ISBN 0-7534-5580-3

Printed in Malaysia

CONTENTS

INTRODUCTION

Nothing beats the thrill of a sudden scientific discovery; and we can appreciate the excitement of an engineer or inventor who solves a tough problem with a single, smart idea. We call such dramatic leaps of knowledge "eureka moments" after the shout of Archimedes (287–212 B.C.). This Greek genius made a bathtime discovery that sent him scampering naked through his city, shouting "Eureka!"—Greek for "I've got it!"

Archimedes had been puzzling over a tricky problem. The king, Hiero II, had given a craftsman a block of precious gold to make a crown. When it was finished, the crown weighed the same as the block, but the king suspected the goldsmith had switched some gold for cheaper silver. Hiero told Archimedes to prove he had been cheated—or die!

Archimedes was pondering the problem as he stepped into a full bathtub. The bath overflowed, and he realized that the volume of water flowing out was equal to the space his body took up.

Louis Daguerre (see pages 56–57), when congratulated on his invention of photography, had a glum reply: "You must not forget that this discovery only happened after 11 years of discouraging experiments, which had dampened my spirits."

! EUREKA! Archimedes could use the same idea to test the crown. He knew that if the crown was pure gold, it would take up the same space as a gold block of equal weight. But silver is lighter than gold: a block of silver the same weight as the pure gold block would be twice as big. So a crown of mixed metals would take up more room than a pure gold one. To test the crown he lowered a block of pure gold that was the same weight as the crown into a bowl of water. Next he swapped the block for the crown. If it was pure gold, the water would fill the bowl exactly as before. But when he lowered in the crown, some water overflowed.

Archimedes had proven that the crown was a mixture of gold and silver. The clever test had saved his life!

Few other scientists have so much at stake, but this does not reduce their excitement when they find what they have been searching for.

Archimedes was famous for his ideas about why objects float or sink and for figuring out the space that curved objects take up . . . and much more.

It did not take a eureka moment to invent the Walkman. Sony head Masura Ibuka thought of it and relied on a team of engineers to create the mini tape player (see pages 86–87).

Eureka moments do not take the sweat out of invention. Orville Wright had one, but it still took him and his brother Wilbur another four years to build the world's first aircraft (see pages 48–49).

The stories in this book are memorable because they make science and technology interesting and help remind us of great discoveries. We remember them precisely because they are unusual. But only a few scientific discoveries are made this way. Today our world is so complex that scientists cannot always solve problems on their own. They work in teams or combine many older inventions to make something new. So at the end of the book you can read how some familiar (and some peculiar) ideas developed without a shout of "Eureka!" and a naked dash outside.

EVERYDAY LIFE AND HEALTH

Legendary eureka moments help us understand the
genius of a few of the most famous figures in science:
Galileo and Newton. But moments of creativity have
also helped less famous scientists make important
discoveries that affect our everyday life and health.
These people played a part in the invention of some
handy gadgets that make our lives much easier.

THE PENDULUM

Clocks first ticked and tocked around 700 years ago, but they did not keep very good time. Few were accurate enough to measure minutes, so they just had one hand that showed the hours. Minute hands appeared only in the 1600s after Italian medical student Galileo Galilei had a brilliant idea during a very boring church service.

But who was Galileo Galilei?

Born in 1564, Galilei (d. 1642)—usually referred to as Galileo—was the son of a music teacher from Pisa, Italy. After failing to become a monk he went to Pisa University, where his awkward questions won him many enemies. Galileo became interested in how objects moved and fell. Later he became famous by using a telescope (see pages 54–55) to prove that Earth moved around the Sun. Religious leaders (who mistakenly believed the opposite) imprisoned him for this.

Galileo's eureka moment

Galileo must have seen it swinging hundreds of times before, but it was not until his first year as a medical student that he really noticed the thurible (an incense burner) in Pisa's cathedral. A monk was swinging it to spread the smoke from incense burning inside. Galileo timed the swings using his pulse—the regular heartbeat throb he could feel on his wrist. To his surprise each swing, big or small, took exactly the same number of beats. Galileo then tried some experiments swinging pendulums—weights on different lengths of string.

EUREKA! Galileo found that the weight made no difference to the swing time. Instead the length of the pendulum did.

Galileo suggested that a swinging pendulum could alternately catch and release the jagged teeth on a clock's cogwheel, keeping it turning at a constant speed. His son tried to build this type of pendulum clock (reconstructed here), but he did not live long enough to complete it.

There are many stories about the moment Galileo had his great pendulum idea in the cathedral. Some believe he watched a monk light a chandelier of candles and then release it. But what Pisans still call "Galileo's lamp" is actually an incense burner.

Keeping time

Doubling the length made the swings take four times as long, and cutting the length in half quartered the time. Galileo suggested to his teachers that doctors could use a specifically marked pendulum to measure a patient's pulse. Disease speeds up the pulse, so doctors routinely check it. Galileo's device—a pulsilogium—helped them measure it exactly.

However, it was not until Galileo was 77 years old—and completely blind—that he thought about using the pendulum's even swing to keep a clock running smoothly. His son, Vicenzo (1606–1649), sketched the pendulum clock his father described to him. After Galileo died Vicenzo made a model—but he could not make it tick. It was a Dutch scientist, Christian Huygens (1629–1695), who built the world's first working pendulum clock in 1656.

Galileo's eureka moment kept the world running on time for almost three centuries. Pendulums swung inside most clocks until the invention of the electronic clock in 1929.

To ensure that the bell inside Big Ben rings on time this huge clock in London, England, has a 13-ft.-long pendulum. The clock's maker built a special mechanism into it to keep it running on time, even when pigeons perch on the hands.

THE THEORY OF GRAVITY

When we drop something, why does it always fall down and not fly off in some other direction? English scientist Isaac Newton was the first to explain gravity, the force that gives objects weight, keeps our feet on the ground, and stops the universe from flying apart. According to legend, inspiration came to him in 1665 in the most famous eureka moment of all time.

But who was Isaac Newton?

Brought up by his grandmother, Isaac Newton (1642–1727) devised ingenious toys as a child. By day he made mouse-powered machines; by night he lifted lanterns into the sky on kites. He grew up to be a proud, argumentative genius who made discoveries—about mathematics, movement, force, and color—that we still use today.

Cuttings from Newton's tree still grow in orchards in southeast England. A piece of fruit just like this triggered his eureka moment.

Newton's eureka moment

One day late in the summer the scientist was deep in thought when a falling apple caught his attention: "Why does the apple never fall up or to the side?" He guessed that some invisible force must be pulling the apple toward the center of Earth.

! EUREKA! Newton realized that the force, which he called gravity, draws together not just apples and Earth but all objects. It could even explain why Earth orbits the Sun instead of flying off into outer space.

Without gravity the Moon would travel in a straight line. The huge masses of Earth and the Moon create a strong gravitational pull. This draws them together, just as Earth's mass draws an apple toward it. This force makes the Moon constantly "fall" toward Earth, changing its straight route through space into an ellipse (a flattened circle).

Newton's famous
tree grew on the grounds of his home
in Lincolnshire, England. According
to some versions of the story, the apple
hit him on the head. This detail was
probably added later to make the tale
more entertaining, but the rest is true.
Newton himself told several
friends the story.

Taking it further

Newton thought more
about gravity and was able to
explain its characteristics in his universal
theory of gravitation. This showed that the
force of gravity pulls all objects together. Its
strength is in proportion to the mass of the
object. But distance reduces the force:
objects twice as far apart are attracted
with one fourth of the gravity.

Today researchers measure gravity with equipment such
as this torsion pendulum. Moving heavy balls closer
slows the swing of a pendulum inside the central tube.

THE COTTON GIN

While staying at a cotton plantation American science teacher Eli Whitney watched slaves struggle to separate seeds from cotton fibers. Careful observation in 1794—and an inventive streak—led him to build a labor-saving machine to do the same job. His cotton gin changed the course of American history, spreading slavery throughout the South.

But who was Eli Whitney?

Eli Whitney (1765–1825) was a farmer's son. As a boy he was smart and inventive: he made a violin at the age of 14 and sold nails he made in the family forge one year later. After studying law and science at Yale University Whitney moved south to become a teacher. He turned to inventing in 1793 when his teaching job fell through.

Whitney's eureka moment

Whitney was staying with cotton farmer Catherine Greene. The cotton that grew on her inland plantation (below) had short fibers that took a long time to separate from the seeds. Cotton grown on the coast had long fibers and was much quicker to process. Greene explained that even when using black slaves to do the work, it was still hard for her to compete. The problem sparked Whitney's imagination. He dreamed of inventing a machine to do the job.

EUREKA! The answer came in a flash. Wires placed in a spinning drum could pull the fibers through a comb that was too fine for the seeds to pass through.

Building the gin

Whitney described his machine to Phineas Miller, the young manager of the estate. Intrigued, Miller offered to pay him to build the gin (engine) in exchange for half of the profit. Within ten days Whitney had made a small model—with it one slave could do the work of ten others cleaning cotton by hand. The two partners were delighted. Whitney quickly patented his invention in 1794—making it illegal for anyone to copy it. He then started making cotton gins in a workshop in New Haven, Connecticut. But the partners did not sell the machines. Instead they processed the farmers' crops, keeping some of the cleaned cotton as a fee. It seemed like a clever scheme, but the machine was so simple that anyone who had seen it in operation immediately understood how it worked. Planters ignored the patent, copied the gin, and cleaned their own cotton. Within three years the business collapsed.

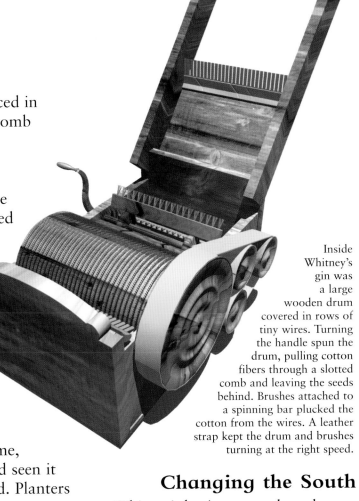

Inside Whitney's gin was a large wooden drum covered in rows of tiny wires. Turning the handle spun the drum, pulling cotton fibers through a slotted comb and leaving the seeds behind. Brushes attached to a spinning bar plucked the cotton from the wires. A leather strap kept the drum and brushes turning at the right speed.

Farmers still grow cotton in the southern states, but they have much bigger machines than Whitney's cotton gin to help them with their harvests. Slavery is now illegal in the U.S., and all workers are paid for their time.

Changing the South

Whitney's business may have been a failure, but his invention certainly was not. It helped spread cotton fields from the southeast coast to plantations far inland. Farmers who illegally copied the gin became very rich. To operate the machines—and to plant and harvest the crops—they brought thousands of slaves from Africa, often forcing them to live in terrible conditions. This expansion of slavery, which many Americans thought was cruel and wrong, led to the Civil War in 1861.

In contrast to the slaves' misery, Whitney quickly recovered from his business disappointment. He won a contract supplying guns to the U.S. government, pioneering new manufacturing methods and machines. He died a wealthy man in 1825.

VACCINATION

There is nothing small about smallpox. This deadly disease once killed one tenth of all children in Great Britain. Folk remedies helped protect a few of them, but it was a young dairymaid's bragging that led English doctor Edward Jenner to a safe remedy. Because of his vaccination discovery in 1788, no one today dies of smallpox.

But who was Edward Jenner?

Edward Jenner (1749–1823), the son of a priest, was born in the village of Berkeley, England. From the ages of 13 to 21 he worked as an assistant surgeon and then studied medicine in London before returning home as a doctor.

And what exactly was smallpox?

The disease started with a high fever and a bright red rash and sometimes killed those infected within two days. Oozing "pocks" (blisters) scarred those lucky enough to survive longer. Smallpox was a horrible disease.

To infect eight-year-old James Phipps with cowpox Jenner made several cuts on the boy's arm. He then rubbed in some of the puss he had taken from blisters on the hand of a patient.

Traditional cures

Edward Jenner knew about many traditional cures when he became a village doctor in 1773. He had heard how people protected their children by rubbing puss from a smallpox blister into skin scratches, but he also knew that this "treatment" often passed on the disease instead of stopping it.

Jenner's eureka moment

It was dairymaid Sarah Nelmes who gave Jenner the idea of how he might control smallpox. He heard her brag that she could not get smallpox because she once caught a much less serious disease—cowpox—from the cows she milked.

EUREKA! A smallpox outbreak in 1788 proved she was right. Jenner's patients who had caught cowpox did not get smallpox.

Testing the theory

Jenner decided to prove that cowpox protected people from smallpox. He would have to infect a healthy person with the killer disease. In 1796 Jenner found the courage to try it out.

Injecting a vaccine into a vein gives our bodies a harmless, mild dose of a disease from which we need protection. Our white cells "remember" the infection and react quickly and strongly when the real, dangerous smallpox germs attack.

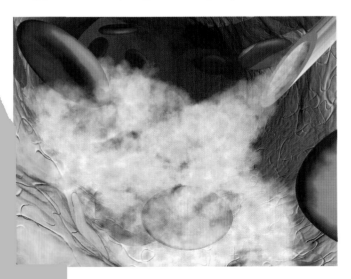

Today Jenner's vaccination method protects us against many dangerous diseases. Instead of cowpox medical workers inject a specifically weakened form of the disease into the patient.

Jenner chose his gardener's son, James Phipps, and carefully infected the boy with cowpox—using puss from the blisters of another patient. Phipps got a slight fever, but he soon recovered. Seven weeks later Jenner did the experiment again—this time using puss from a smallpox sufferer. To Jenner's relief Phipps did not get the disease. The cowpox had made the boy immune to (unable to catch) smallpox.

What happened next?

Doctors were not convinced of Jenner's treatment, which he called vaccination. Great Britain's Royal Society of Medicine would not report his discovery, so Jenner published a book about it. Then vaccination became popular. A new law introduced in 1845 forced everyone to be vaccinated. And by 1980 a huge vaccination program killed off smallpox everywhere in the world. But scientists have now suggested that terrorist organizations could reintroduce diseases such as smallpox, and these diseases may be genetically modified and thus able to resist vaccines.

READY-MADE BUILDINGS

Putting together a building from ready-made parts makes instant construction possible. The first structure built like this was London, England's Crystal Palace in 1851. Joseph Paxton's idea for its thin steel girders and huge windows came from an unlikely source—the bottom of a giant water lily.

But who was Joseph Paxton?

The son of a poor English farmer, Joseph Paxton (1803–1865) ran away from home to escape hunger and abuse. By lying about his age he got a job as a gardener on a rich man's estate. There he became a skilled botanist (plant expert) and took control of the greenhouses.

The monster lily

Paxton was given a tiny sample of a water lily that grew to an enormous size in its natural habitat—South America. He planted it in a heated pool inside a greenhouse. The water lily's leaves swelled to 5 ft. (1.5m)—big enough for Paxton's seven-year-old daughter to stand on. The lily soon outgrew the greenhouse, and Paxton wondered how he could build a new one. It needed to have plenty of glass with very few girders blocking the light.

Paxton knew nothing about the strength of glass and iron. He relied on engineers Fox, Henderson, and Company to make sure that every part of the building—such as these huge central arches—would not fall down.

In the 25 weeks that it was open Crystal Palace attracted huge crowds. Then it was taken down, moved 7.5 mi., and rebuilt— in a different shape!

Paxton's eureka moment

The water lily itself gave Paxton the answer. Turning over one of the leaves, he gazed at the strong ribs that spread out from the stem that held up the leaf's surface.

EUREKA! Paxton realized he could make a strong, lightweight building using iron and glass by copying nature.

What happened next?

Paxton built his lily house, and two years later he got the chance to build a bigger, grander version. A festival of art and industry was planned in a park in London, England. After a committee rejected 245 designs for the exhibition hall Paxton sent in a plan. Starting with a doodle he designed the world's biggest greenhouse. By using hundreds of cast-iron frames, each the same size and shape, he created a cheap, bolted-together building. Londoners loved it, and the building— nicknamed Crystal Palace—made Paxton the world's favorite gardener.

Once the show was over the building was moved to a new site a few miles away. Though fire destroyed it in 1936, Londoners still call the district where it stood Crystal Palace.

Crystal Palace was built using just a few types of iron parts, endlessly copied. Though the parts were made in three different factories across England, they all matched so that they fit together perfectly.

Today all big buildings use some ready-made parts. This Japanese housing project takes it one step further. Whole bathrooms arrive with the plumbing complete, ready to be bolted into position.

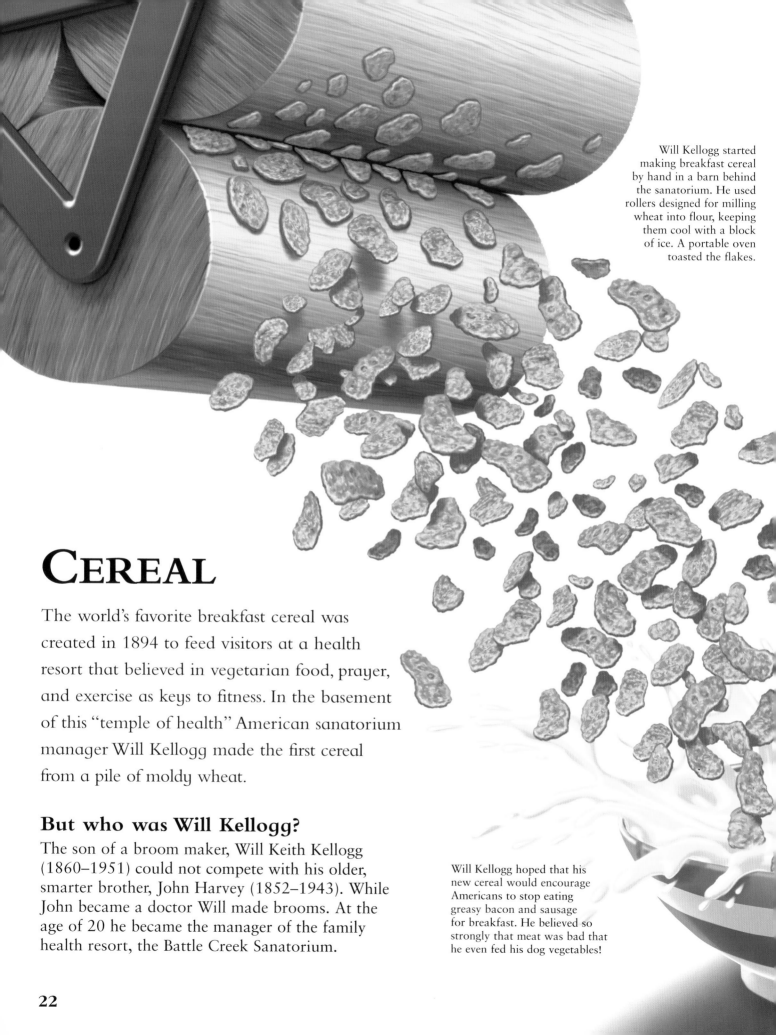

CEREAL

The world's favorite breakfast cereal was created in 1894 to feed visitors at a health resort that believed in vegetarian food, prayer, and exercise as keys to fitness. In the basement of this "temple of health" American sanatorium manager Will Kellogg made the first cereal from a pile of moldy wheat.

But who was Will Kellogg?

The son of a broom maker, Will Keith Kellogg (1860–1951) could not compete with his older, smarter brother, John Harvey (1852–1943). While John became a doctor Will made brooms. At the age of 20 he became the manager of the family health resort, the Battle Creek Sanatorium.

Will Kellogg started making breakfast cereal by hand in a barn behind the sanatorium. He used rollers designed for milling wheat into flour, keeping them cool with a block of ice. A portable oven toasted the flakes.

Will Kellogg hoped that his new cereal would encourage Americans to stop eating greasy bacon and sausage for breakfast. He believed so strongly that meat was bad that he even fed his dog vegetables!

Will Kellogg's eureka moment

While John was the sanatorium's glamorous boss Will managed the accounts and did the chores. One of his jobs included adding variety to the dull vegetarian diet. Experimenting with boiled wheat one night, Will found that it formed a sticky mess when it was crushed between rollers. He left most of the wheat unrolled. In the morning he discovered that the wheat was moldy, but he decided to roll it anyway.

EUREKA! The wheat broke up into flakes when it came out of the rollers. Will repeated the experiment and realized that long soaking (not mold) was the key. Soaked, rolled, and toasted, wheat grains made delicious flakes.

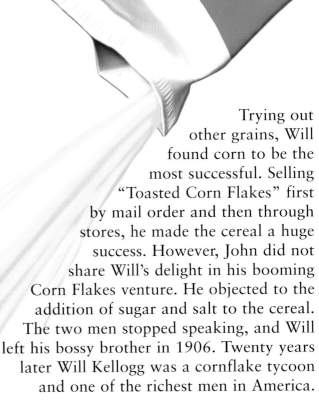

Trying out other grains, Will found corn to be the most successful. Selling "Toasted Corn Flakes" first by mail order and then through stores, he made the cereal a huge success. However, John did not share Will's delight in his booming Corn Flakes venture. He objected to the addition of sugar and salt to the cereal. The two men stopped speaking, and Will left his bossy brother in 1906. Twenty years later Will Kellogg was a cornflake tycoon and one of the richest men in America.

It was advertising that really made Corn Flakes a success. Kellogg had a flair for slogans and marketing gimmicks, promising housewives a free sample if they winked at their grocer.

"Oh! Look Who's Here"

TOASTED CORN FLAKES

MADE FROM SELECTED WHITE CORN. NONE GENUINE WITHOUT THIS SIGNATURE

W. K. Kellogg

KELLOGG TOASTED CORN FLAKE CO., Battle Creek, Mich.
Canadian Trade Supplied by the Battle Creek Toasted Corn Flake Co., Ltd., London, Ont.

THE VACUUM CLEANER

One hundred years ago cleaning a carpet meant lifting it off of the floor, carrying it outside, and beating it until all the dirt fell out. It was hard, dirty work, and engineer Hubert Booth was sure there must be an easier, cleaner way to do it. When he discovered there was not, he invented one in 1901—and almost choked on the dust!

But who was Hubert Booth?

Hubert Cecil Booth (1871–1955) was a British engineer who designed bridges, battleships, and Ferris wheels (see right). But it is for vacuum cleaners and the labor-saving contribution they made to house cleaning that he is now remembered.

Booth designed Ferris wheels in Blackpool, England; Paris, France; and Vienna, Austria. The first two have now been demolished, but you can still ride on his Vienna wheel— the Riesenrad (giant wheel). Built in 1897, it stands in the Prater amusement park and is 210 ft. across.

Booth's eureka moment

Booth went to watch an American inventor show off a machine that blew dust off of the seats of railroad cars. It certainly worked: the jet of compressed air blew clouds of filth off of the cushions—and into the faces of everyone watching. Booth asked the inventor why the machine could not suck up the dirt, but he was told that this approach did not work.

Booth did not believe this, so he placed a handkerchief on a chair cushion. Pressing his mouth against it, he took a deep breath and inhaled a lungful of dust! Once he had stopped coughing he turned the handkerchief over.

! **EUREKA!** On the back was a dark ring of dirt where his mouth had been. It was enough to convince Booth that a vacuum cleaner was both practical and possible.

Booth's monster

Booth bought an electric motor and a pump, and in 1901 he built the world's first effective vacuum cleaner. There was one problem—it was too big to fit through the door of a house! However, this did not put his customers off. They held parties so their friends could watch the filth being sucked out of their carpets and swept along flexible hoses to a machine in the street outside. Within seven years other companies had brought out vacuums that were small enough to use indoors, and by 1938 two thirds of all families had thrown away their carpet beaters and were using vacuums.

This early advertisement for a vacuum cleaner shows a maid using it while her mistress watches. But this was not what really happened—more often it was the mistress who operated it herself. Instead of saving women from housework the vacuum cleaner replaced household servants.

Booth did not sell vacuums. Instead he offered a cleaning service. Cleaners passed hoses through the windows and sucked dirt from carpets into this huge machine that was parked outside on the street. The machines were unpopular: they blocked the road and were so noisy that passing horses were frightened.

The cyclone design

After the introduction of small electric models around 1908 vacuum cleaners hardly changed for the rest of the 1900s. The only real improvement was the cyclone design (left). Launched in 1993, it replaced vacuum bags with an efficient "whirlwind" dust separator. This did not get clogged as it filled up, so unlike vacuums with bags the machine kept its sucking power. Clean and slick, these bagless vacuums could not be more different from Booth's huge, noisy monster.

FROZEN FOOD

Today we expect to eat peas in the middle of winter or shrimp that once swam in an ocean on the other side of the world. Freezing and packaging makes our favorite foods available anywhere and at any time of the year. It began with Clarence Birdseye's 1912 discovery in the Arctic, where winter lasts most of the year.

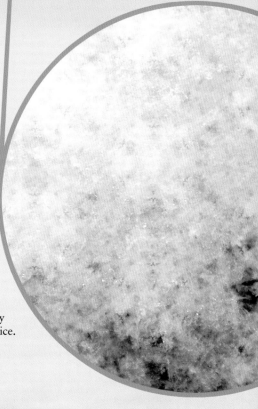

But who was Clarence Birdseye?

Born in Brooklyn, New York, Clarence Birdseye (1886–1956) went to college to study biology but never finished. Instead he worked as a field biologist with the U.S. government and traveled to the frozen north of Canada.

Birdseye's eureka moment

During his travels in Labrador in 1912 Birdseye watched the natives fishing. They chipped holes into the ice covering a lake. The intense cold air instantly froze the fish as it was pulled out.

! EUREKA! Birdseye realized that this quick chilling solved a problem that always spoiled frozen food: ice. Though it may seem strange, the one thing that preserved frozen food also harmed it (see main image for more details).

When food freezes slowly, ice forms in long, sharp crystals. The crystals stab through the food like knives, cutting it apart from the inside. When slow-frozen food thaws, it turns to mush. But Birdseye found out that rapid freezing keeps crystals small, thus not harming the insides of the fish. So quick-frozen fish tastes as good six months later as the day it was first put on the ice.

Building an Arctic factory

Birdseye realized that getting frozen food into America's kitchens was not going to be easy. He would have to find a way to stop food from thawing on the way to the store. It took him eight years to figure out how to chill the food fast enough to keep the daggers of ice from forming. By 1923 he had invented a machine that squeezed prepackaged food between two very cold plates, but it took him until 1930 to solve the rest of the problems.

Unless they planned to eat frozen food the same day, families needed freezers, and few had them. In the 1930s even refrigerators were uncommon: two million U.S. homes had one, but in Great Britain there were only 3,000. Freezers became common kitchen appliances in the U.S. in the 1950s and much later in Europe.

Fish sticks

In Europe fish sticks got families hooked on frozen food. They were launched in 1955 as "a new, delicious way to buy fish, which takes the time, trouble, and smell out of preparing one of our favorite foods." It had taken almost 50 years, but Birdseye's brilliant idea was finally a tremendous success. Although Birdseye's name appears on millions of packages of frozen food, he was never proud of his achievement, commenting, "I do not consider myself a remarkable person. I am just a guy with a very large bump of curiosity."

Birdseye's frozen food came in a solid block that was slow to thaw and inconvenient to cook. In modern freezer plants a blast of icy air freezes the food, keeping it from sticking together. Here workers check fish sticks before they are frozen and packaged.

ANTIBIOTICS

Thanks to a lucky accident in 1928, Scottish doctor Alexander Fleming discovered one of medicine's most powerful weapons in the fight against germs: penicillin. However, he failed to realize its true value. The lifesaving mold was turned into a drug only after Australian researcher Howard Florey stumbled on Fleming's findings in a dusty library.

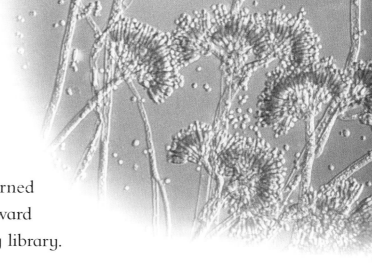

Fleming's lifesaving mold was similar to the many molds that grow on old food. Magnified hundreds of times under the microscope, penicillium looks like a flower with a brush-shaped top.

But who were Fleming and Florey?

Alexander Fleming (1881–1955) studied medicine in London, England. As an army doctor in World War I (1914–1918) he watched soldiers die from common infections. When peace returned, he searched for new antiseptic drugs.

Howard Florey (1898–1968) was a clever Australian who shared Fleming's interest in germ-killing drugs. By 1935 he was a professor of pathology (the cause of diseases) at Oxford University in England.

Fleming's report

Fleming studied the mold (which he called penicillium) for awhile. By injecting some into a healthy rabbit he proved that it was not harmful. But he did not take the next step—using a sick rabbit to check how good the mold was at curing diseases. Instead he simply published details of his discovery in the *British Journal of Experimental Pathology*.

Fleming's eureka moment

Alexander Fleming was a brilliant scientist, but he was messy in the laboratory. When he went away on vacation in 1928, he left behind a pile of failed experiments—jelly-filled glass dishes in which he grew bacteria. When he returned, he went to wash them out and noticed that one dish stood out from the others. A patch of mold had grown on it, and a circle of jelly around the mold was free of bacteria.

EUREKA! Fleming realized that the mold was killing the bacteria. He thought that it might be a way of curing the diseases that bacteria cause.

Mass production of penicillin began only when it was needed to save the lives of soldiers wounded in World War II.

From mold to drug

Oxford University professor Howard Florey and his assistant, Ernst Chain (1906–1979), were researching in the same field as Fleming—his article was one of 200 they read in 1939. Unlike Fleming, their research team had the know-how to extract and purify the healing agent from the mold. They tested it on eight mice, each infected with a deadly disease. Only the four treated with the (newly named) penicillin survived.

Nobel Prize winners

The lab became a penicillin factory, but the team could still not make useful quantities of the drug. Only when the United States government became interested and agreed to manufacture large quantities of penicillin was Florey able to test it properly. Penicillin—the first of a group of drugs we call antibiotics—proved to be a lifesaver. For its development Fleming, Florey, and Chain shared the Nobel Prize in Medicine in 1945.

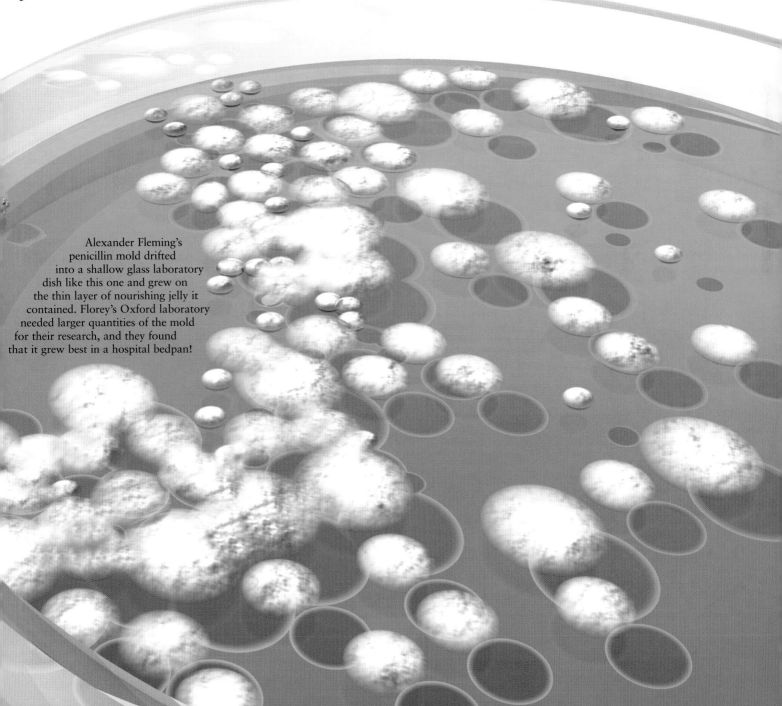

Alexander Fleming's penicillin mold drifted into a shallow glass laboratory dish like this one and grew on the thin layer of nourishing jelly it contained. Florey's Oxford laboratory needed larger quantities of the mold for their research, and they found that it grew best in a hospital bedpan!

NYLON

In the 1930s U.S. a chemical company decided to invent a substitute for silk. They hired a team of bright young chemists to help them. Fooling around while the boss, Wallace Carothers, was away, the scientists invented one of today's best-known fibers.

But who was Wallace Carothers?

Eccentric genius Wallace Carothers (1896–1937) was such a smart college student that he was made head of the chemistry department before he had even graduated. As a professor at Harvard University he studied the structure of plastic until the giant chemical company DuPont hired him in 1928.

"Get rid of the worms, Carothers!"

DuPont wanted Carothers to make a substitute for silk. This fine, expensive fiber is spun by silkworms—the larvae of Chinese moths. Carothers began working and hired eight assistants.

Years after the stretching experiment Julian Hill acted out the moment when he drew the first threads from the sticky mass in his test tube. It is the action of pulling and extending nylon that gives this plastic its great strength.

Under the watchful eye of their leader the team created polymers—plastics with a chainlike structure that made them immensely strong. Their first breakthrough was *neoprene*, a kind of synthetic rubber. A few weeks later they made another plastic, nicknamed *3-16 polymer*, that looked very promising. Carothers instructed an assistant, Julian Hill (1904–1996), to do most of the work on *3-16 polymer*.

Polymers, such as nylon, are created using organic chemicals—substances made by living things. Squeezing and heating the chemicals makes their structure change from liquids and gases into strong solids. If you could see inside a polymer, you would notice that its atoms (tiniest particles) are arranged in long, very stretchy chains.

The team's eureka moment

One day in 1930 while Carothers was out of the lab Hill dipped a stirring rod into a tube of the white, sticky plastic and found that he could pull out a thread. The thread of plastic was very stretchy and strong, so Hill and his colleagues staged a tug-of-war in the hall to see just how far they could pull it. To their amazement stretching the threads of plastic made them even stronger.

The first nylon socks wrinkled badly, but women did not care because they were much tougher than silk. DuPont could not make them fast enough, and people fought to get the few pairs available.

EUREKA! These plastic threads were just as springy as silk, and they could be made from oil, water, and air without the aid of moths.

What happened next?

But *3-16 polymer* turned out to be useless for making clothes. Ironing melted it! Carothers and his team tried for four years to find other ways to make plastic clothing fibers. When none worked, they returned to *3-16 polymer*. By altering the recipe in 1934 they made a handful of the "artificial silk" that DuPont wanted. After five more years of research factories were able to produce large quantities of the newly named nylon.

TEFLON

In his laboratory at DuPont American scientist Roy Plunkett was trying to invent new cooling fluids for refrigerators and air conditioners in 1938. He had filled a gas tank with a coolant and chilled it to an icy -110°F (-79°C). But when he opened the valve the next day to release the gas, nothing came out. What happened next changed clothing, cooking, and manufacturing forever.

But who was Roy Plunkett?

Chemist Roy Plunkett (1910–1994) joined giant American chemical company DuPont straight out of college. He had been with the firm only two years when he made his lucky discovery in 1938. He worked for DuPont for the rest of his life, where his jobs included adding lead to gasoline.

Plunkett's eureka moment

When nothing came out of the tank during the cooling-fluid experiment, Plunkett and his assistant thought the tank had leaked. They put it on a scale, but it weighed the same as it did when it was full. The valve was not clogged, and when they unscrewed it, white waxy flakes fell out. Finally they sawed the tank in half. Inside it was coated with the same slippery white material. This plasticlike substance had one extraordinary property: it did absolutely nothing!

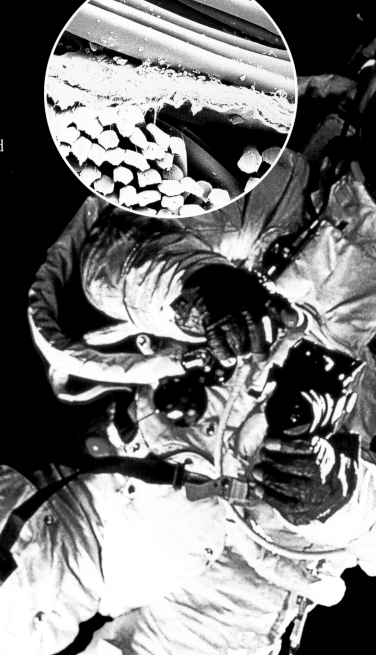

Astronauts who flew to the Moon as part of the U.S. Apollo program wore thick pressure suits made from 25 layers of fabric and plastic. The outer layer, made from pure Teflon fibers, stopped the suit from rubbing and protected it against fire. Two lower layers were also Teflon-coated, as shown in the close-up image.

EUREKA! Plunkett had made the dullest, slipperiest, most unreactive substance ever known. Nothing affected the new chemical.

The dullest substance on Earth

The gas Plunkett had started with had the tongue-twisting name tetrafluoroethylene (TFE). He guessed that the tiny gas molecules had joined to make a long chain called a polymer. So Plunkett named it "polytetrafluoroethylene" (PTFE). Later DuPont called it Teflon. However, slipperiness is a surprisingly useful quality. Teflon could make things slip easily without using oil. It could protect surfaces that were under chemical attack. One of its first uses was on the Manhattan Project, America's top secret plan to build an atomic bomb.

To test his invention Plunkett raided his laboratory cupboard. He attacked the PTFE with searing acids, powerful chemicals, and nasty liquids that dissolved almost anything. He heated it. He froze it. And still the shiny white plastic looked like new. In this recreation of one of his tests the chemist dips a plastic rod and a Teflon rod into acid. As Plunkett found the acid will dissolve the plastic but will not affect the Teflon.

Nonstick pans were the idea of Frenchwoman Collette Grégoire. Her husband, Marc, planned to use Teflon to stop his fishing gear from getting tangled, but Collette suggested nonstick pans would be more useful. Calling the coating "Tefal," they started production in 1954. This early French advertisement said, "Nothing sticks to Tefal."

From frying pans to human hearts

Peaceful uses for Teflon soon followed. When the United States began sending astronauts into space and later to the Moon, Teflon-coated fibers protected their space suits. Back on Earth Teflon coatings made nonstick frying pans so cooks could fry without using butter or oil. Today there is probably some Teflon in your clothing to protect it from moisture, dirt, and stains. People who have heart surgery wear Teflon inside their bodies! It is perfect for "knitting" together artificial blood vessels. Unlike other materials, it does not cause a harmful reaction, so human tissue grows into the fabric as if it were part of the patient.

THE MICROWAVE OVEN

Puzzled by a chocolate bar melting in his pocket, ingenious American engineer Percy Spencer used the throbbing heart of a wartime radar to pop corn and boil eggs. During World War II he invented a whole new way of cooking, kept his factory from closing, and saved the jobs of thousands of workers.

But who was Percy Spencer?

American orphan Percy Lebaron Spencer (1894–1970) never finished high school, but this did not hold back his inventive nature. By the time World War II (1939–1945) broke out he was a senior engineer with electronics company Raytheon.

Percy Spencer wins the war

British engineers asked Raytheon to help them detect and stop bomber aircraft flying from Germany, Great Britain's wartime foe. The engineers had developed radar (right), which spotted the planes using microwaves—special radio waves. However, each radar set needed a device, called a magnetron, to generate the microwaves, and British factories could not make them fast enough.

Raytheon put Spencer on the job, and in one weekend he had figured out how to make magnetrons more quickly. Raytheon's factory was soon making magnetrons 150 times faster than they were made before.

Spencer's eureka moment

Spencer was testing a magnetron one day when he noticed something strange. A chocolate bar in his pocket had melted. He immediately realized that the microwaves from the magnetron had heated it up. Spencer sent an assistant to buy some dry corn, and he put this right in front of the magnetron. Switching on the power turned it instantly into popcorn.

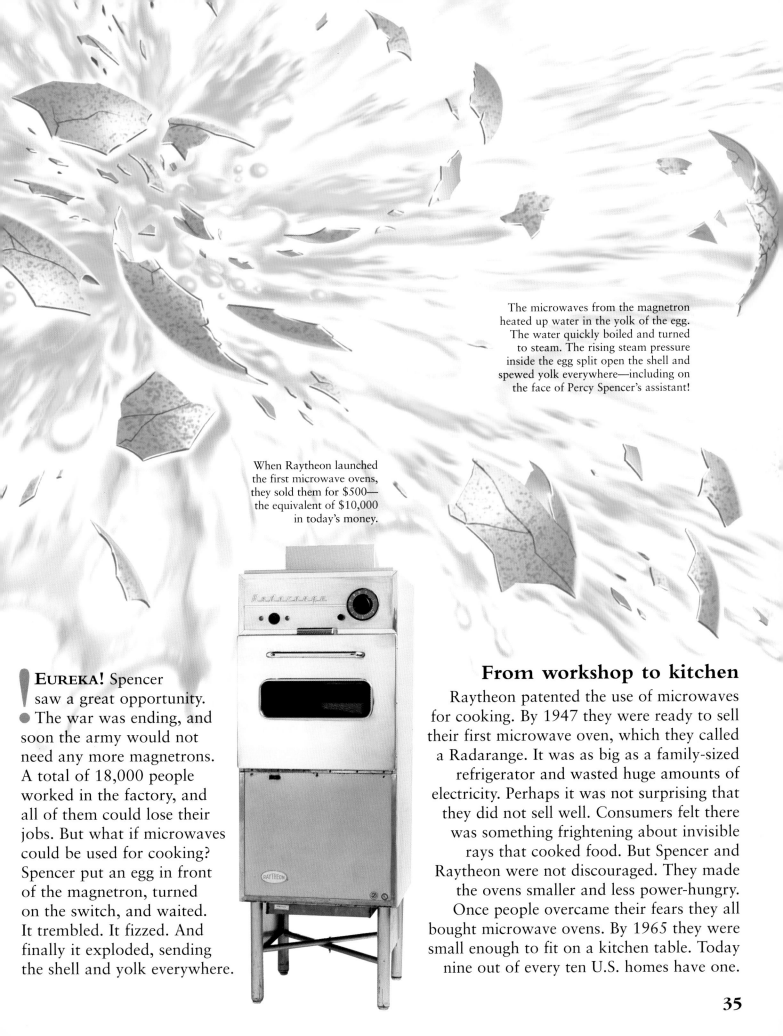

The microwaves from the magnetron heated up water in the yolk of the egg. The water quickly boiled and turned to steam. The rising steam pressure inside the egg split open the shell and spewed yolk everywhere—including on the face of Percy Spencer's assistant!

When Raytheon launched the first microwave ovens, they sold them for $500— the equivalent of $10,000 in today's money.

EUREKA! Spencer saw a great opportunity. The war was ending, and soon the army would not need any more magnetrons. A total of 18,000 people worked in the factory, and all of them could lose their jobs. But what if microwaves could be used for cooking? Spencer put an egg in front of the magnetron, turned on the switch, and waited. It trembled. It fizzed. And finally it exploded, sending the shell and yolk everywhere.

From workshop to kitchen

Raytheon patented the use of microwaves for cooking. By 1947 they were ready to sell their first microwave oven, which they called a Radarange. It was as big as a family-sized refrigerator and wasted huge amounts of electricity. Perhaps it was not surprising that they did not sell well. Consumers felt there was something frightening about invisible rays that cooked food. But Spencer and Raytheon were not discouraged. They made the ovens smaller and less power-hungry. Once people overcame their fears they all bought microwave ovens. By 1965 they were small enough to fit on a kitchen table. Today nine out of every ten U.S. homes have one.

DNA FINGERPRINTING

Guilty! A murderer is led away to jail, trapped by DNA fingerprinting. This powerful technology helps crime scientists identify a villain from a tiny speck of their blood or a root of their hair. Alec Jeffreys, the British scientist who invented it, vividly remembers the fall morning in 1984 when he made the discovery that would transform crime investigation forever.

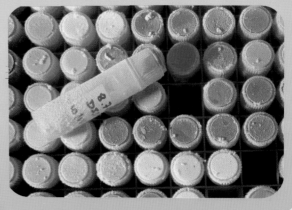

Crime samples waiting to be analyzed may hold the key to who committed the crime. And since our DNA never changes detectives can use it to catch villains years after the crime took place.

But who is Alec Jeffreys?

For an eighth birthday present Alec Jeffreys (1950–) received a chemistry set and a microscope. The gifts led to some dangerous experiments, but they also sparked a serious interest in science. He studied biochemistry and genetics at Oxford University in England.

A stammer that identifies us all

Jeffreys went to work at Leicester University in England. There he began experimenting with DNA, the long molecule that contains the genetic code (see pages 38–39). Jeffreys' team was searching for ways to spot and stop inherited diseases. These rare illnesses run in the family: people get them from their parents and pass them on to their children. Jeffreys noticed a strange quirk of DNA. In parts of it one of the four chemical "letters" from which the code is made was repeated over and over, like a stammer or a stuck CD. Also, unlike most of the genetic code, these repeated letters were always different. No two people had the exact same pattern.

Inside most of our cells is the spiraling, ladderlike DNA molecule. Pairs of chemical letters are its rungs. Their order makes DNA work like a biological computer code, describing everything about us. Half of our DNA is copied from each of our parents, and the study of this transfer of DNA is called genetics.

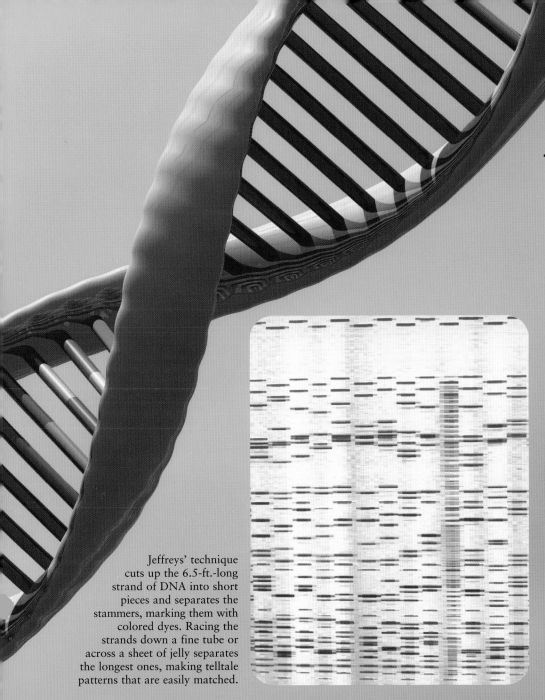

Jeffreys' eureka moment

The importance of this discovery occurred to Jeffreys on Monday, September 15, 1984. He was in a darkroom lifting a piece of photographic film from the developing solution.

! **EUREKA!** He suddenly realized that if the pattern on the film was different for everybody, it could be used to identify them. "It was so obvious . . . " he remembers, " . . . we had stumbled on a way of establishing a human's genetic identification. By the afternoon we had named our discovery DNA fingerprinting."

Jeffreys' technique cuts up the 6.5-ft.-long strand of DNA into short pieces and separates the stammers, marking them with colored dyes. Racing the strands down a fine tube or across a sheet of jelly separates the longest ones, making telltale patterns that are easily matched.

Archaeologists also use DNA fingerprinting to trace our ancestors. By studying the DNA of this mummy preserved in the dry, salty sand of Ürümqi in northwest China scientists proved that it was the body of a man whose ancestors traveled from Europe 3,000 years ago.

Solving crimes

Fingerprints are a valuable tool in solving crimes because they are also unique—no two people have the same pattern of ridges on their fingertips. Clever criminals know this and wear gloves, but gloves cannot stop them from leaving traces of DNA. It is hard for a suspect to deny they were involved in a crime if a sample of their DNA matches skin, hair, saliva, or blood found at the crime scene. DNA fingerprinting was first used in 1985 to clear a man wrongly accused of murder. Since then it has become detectives' most important tool in solving crimes.

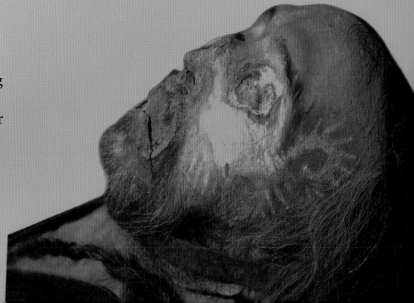

SEQUENCING THE CANCER GENE

When cancer attacks, our bodies lose control of cell growth. Cancer cells multiply, forming a deadly tumor. To find a way to control cell growth—and perhaps cure cancer—researcher Paul Nurse did not study the human body. Instead in 1974 he studied yeast, a tiny organism that carbonates beer.

But who is Paul Nurse?

Born in England in 1949, Paul Nurse became interested in science when he was given a telescope for his eighth birthday, and he used it to look at one of the first spacecraft, *Sputnik II*. Fascinated by birds and plants, he studied biological science at college and then specialized in cell biology.

The cancer gene

Like many other researchers, Nurse studied DNA. This chemical is curled inside most cells of the human body. It is shaped like a twisting ladder. Groups of "rungs" are called genes. Together they provide a construction plan for building a human being, so DNA is sometimes called the "genetic code." For example, there is a gene for brown eyes and another one for red hair. Nurse was looking for a gene that controlled cell growth. Figuring out exactly which gene it is—and how it works— was difficult because humans have up to 400,000 genes. In 1974 he had an idea about how he could make his work easier. What if other living things relied on the same gene to control cell growth? Perhaps by studying something simpler he could figure out what happens in human cells. Nurse chose yeast. This tiny organism has a genetic code that is 80 times simpler than human DNA.

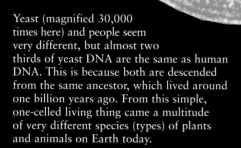

Yeast (magnified 30,000 times here) and people seem very different, but almost two thirds of yeast DNA are the same as human DNA. This is because both are descended from the same ancestor, which lived around one billion years ago. From this simple, one-celled living thing came a multitude of very different species (types) of plants and animals on Earth today.

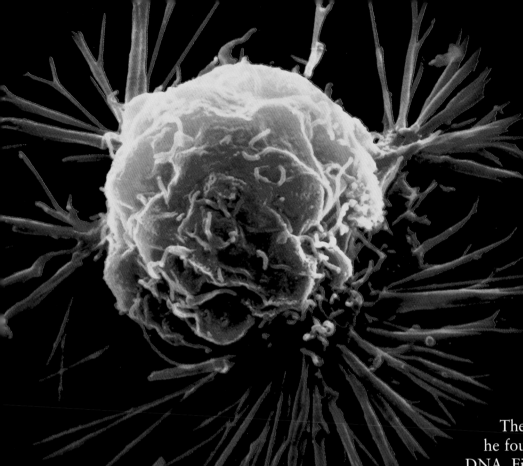

Nurse's eureka moment

When Nurse began working, it seemed like a strange idea. Even he admits that the chances of success were slim. Yet by the early 1980s his team had found the gene that controlled cell growth in yeast. They called it *cdc2*. Soon they had figured out its structure. As Nurse's work continued more and more people began to think that he could be right.

The final test came in 1987 when he found the *cdc2* gene in human DNA. Figuring out its structure was a slow, tedious process. It produced tons of information that meant little until analyzed with a computer. Finally the lab work was complete. All that remained was to let the computer crunch the numbers. As the results trickled in Nurse gazed in astonishment at his computer monitor.

EUREKA! It was just as he had predicted: the yeast and human genes were almost the same. He burst out of his lab and ran through the building spreading the thrilling news.

What happened next?

Modestly, Nurse did not call his work a breakthrough, but it is so important that in 2001 he shared a Nobel Prize—the top award in science. Nurse's research will not lead to an immediate cure for cancer, but it does provide scientists with a valuable new way of studying the disease. Despite many years of research, we still know little about cancer. Helped by Nurse's eureka moment, researchers hope to discover how cancer cells divide out of control and stop them from growing without harming healthy organs.

Cancer cells, like this one, cause harm by damaging surrounding tissues and organs (groups of healthy cells). Understanding how cancerous cells grow is important because one in every three people develops cancer. If we knew more about cancer, we might be able to prevent it by removing what causes it.

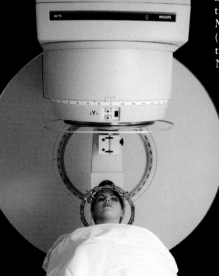

Because we know so little about cancer, modern-day treatments are simple. Most use surgery, radiation (as shown here), or poisons to kill or remove the tumor. Nurse believes that in the future these methods will seem as primitive as shaking a broken clock to try to repair it. He hopes that his work will enable scientists to work like clockmakers so that they really understand what makes the cancer gene tick.

GETTING AROUND

Inventors on the move have turned moments of
fortunate discoveries into an advantage—whether they
were dreaming of soaring like birds or just walking
behind a plow horse. Floating, flying, and hovering all
began with a eureka moment. The one exception was
the safety elevator. The inventor's eureka moment was
a great marketing idea for his invention—rather
than for the invention itself.

THE HOT-AIR BALLOON

The exciting story of air travel began after two French papermakers discovered what they called "electric smoke." From 1783 on they used it to fill huge balloons, and it flew them high up over the rooftops of Paris, France, in the 1800s.

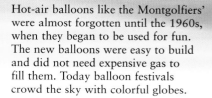

Hot-air balloons like the Montgolfiers' were almost forgotten until the 1960s, when they began to be used for fun. The new balloons were easy to build and did not need expensive gas to fill them. Today balloon festivals crowd the sky with colorful globes.

But who were the Montgolfier brothers?

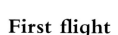

The sons of a wealthy French papermaker, Joseph (1740–1810) and Jacques (1745–1799) Montgolfier were enchanted by the idea of flying. As adults both worked in the family paper business in Annonay, France.

The Montgolfiers' eureka moment

Joseph and Jacques figured out how they could fly while burning some garbage in the kitchen. They noticed that the flames sent scraps of paper floating up the chimney.

! **EUREKA!** If they could only build an aircraft light enough, they could use fire to lift it. They began experimenting, holding bigger and bigger paper bags over a fire to send them floating up. They were excited to discover that each larger bag had more lifting power than the one before it.

First flight

After two years of experiments the Montgolfiers created a globe of fabric lined with paper. It was 33 ft. (10m) wide—almost as big as a circus ring. They launched it on June 5, 1783 in the town square in Annonay, near Lyon, France. The fire they lit underneath the balloon produced such a powerful lifting force that it took eight strong men to hold it down. When they let go, the balloon soared up 5,900 ft. (1,800m). The flight caused a sensation, and three months later the brothers repeated their achievement in front of their king, Louis XVI, in Paris.

Fearing that passengers would be killed, the French king at first insisted that the Montgolfiers' balloon should carry only criminals awaiting execution. But he was persuaded that it was safe, and the first flight (left) carried a doctor, Jean-François Pilâtre de Rozier (1754–1785), and a nobleman, François Laurent, Marquis d'Arlandes (1742–1809).

Hot-air balloons rise because heat makes air expand. This means that the hot air inside the balloon is lighter than the cold air outside of it. The Montgolfier brothers did not know this. They thought the flames and sparks made a special lifting gas that they called "electric smoke."

Smelly smoke

Convinced that smoke lifted their aircraft, they threw old shoes and rotten meat on the fire, creating a stench that drove back the king. The balloon flew for eight minutes, carrying a sheep, a duck, and a cockerel. Though the sheep's kicks injured the cockerel, the animals landed safely.

Soon after the Montgolfier brothers' invention other people filled balloons with hydrogen gas. These gas balloons turned out to be more useful than hot-air balloons. Here (above) a soldier uses one to monitor the battlefields of France during World War I (1914–1918).

People can fly!

Success made the Montgolfier brothers bolder, and by November 1783 they had built another balloon equipped with its own fire and a much bigger basket. The new balloon rose into the skies above Paris on November 21, and it carried two passengers 5.5 mi. (9km). At last humans could fly like birds!

Hot-air balloons made history again in 1999. The *Breitling Orbiter 3* used a combination of helium gas and hot air to carry its crew of two around the world. The three-week flight won the pilots a prize of $1,000,000.

SAFETY ELEVATOR

Sometimes a great invention is not enough on its own—as American Elisha Otis found out. Though his crash-proof elevators saved lives, nobody bought them. Success only came when, in a eureka moment in 1853, he thought of a way to show people just how safe his invention was. Then he could not build them quickly enough to satisfy public demand!

But who was Elisha Otis?

Farmer's son Elisha Graves Otis (1811–1861) drifted from job to job until he found steady work as a mechanic in a bed factory. There he devised several cunning inventions to make machines safer and better. A problem with a cargo elevator in a bed factory in New York City led to the invention that made him famous and made skyscrapers possible.

Dangerous hoists

In 1852 American factories used cargo hoists—simple elevators—to raise goods to upper floors. All suffered from the same problem. If the rope broke, the elevator dropped like a stone, killing anyone onboard. No wonder factory workers feared them.

A new safety device

All factory workers demanded double pay to ride in the car with the cargo. So when his employer began building a new hoist, Otis looked for ways to make the elevator less dangerous. The safety device he invented was simple but effective. It stopped the car's fall after just a few inches. When the bed manufacturer he worked for went bankrupt, Otis set up his own hoist company. But he soon ran into trouble. Nobody was ordering his safety elevators.

The safety hoist was a strong spring attached to the elevator rope. In normal use the elevator car's weight squashed the spring flat, but if the rope broke, the spring curved down, moving two levers that forced "claws" out from the sides of the car. The claws caught a jagged track inside the shaft and stopped the elevator from falling.

Today's tallest skyscrapers would not exist without elevators, which zoom up 60 floors in seconds. Though Otis' safety invention is no longer in use, elevators have similar devices to prevent a death plunge.

Otis staged his demonstration in a tall building called the Latting Observatory, located north of the 1853–1854 World's Fair in New York City. At the end of his dramatic performance Otis took off his hat and bowed as the audience applauded wildly. By repeating the stunt several times each day Otis drew attention to the danger of elevators—and the importance of his invention.

Otis' eureka moment

While musing over the fact that hardly any safety hoists were selling Otis figured out an amazing advertising stunt.

EUREKA! A great exhibition was planned in New York City—Otis realized it would be the perfect place to show off his invention. At the show he set up a steam-powered elevator that climbed up four floors. When a crowd gathered, he jumped inside and rode to the top. There, while he explained the safety features of his new elevator, a man with an ax cut the rope. Screams rose from the audience, but the car hardly dropped before the safety mechanism stopped it. Inside Otis calmed the crowd. "All safe, gentlemen!" he shouted.

What happened next?

Orders rolled in, and Otis built 15 hoists in 1855. Surprisingly, he did not think about lifting people. A customer suggested this in 1856, and Otis' first passenger elevator began operating the next year. Until Otis' invention few buildings were taller than five floors because climbing stairs any higher was exhausting. But with an elevator, the sky was the limit, and the result is the skyscrapers we know today.

THE STUMP-JUMP PLOW

Turning forests into fields was more than most Australian farmers in the 1800s could handle. Many left their farms after tree stumps in the soil ruined their plows and injured their horses. But Richard Smith was not so easily discouraged. A broken plow got him thinking . . .

But who was Richard Smith?

Richard Smith (1837–1919) was still a baby when his parents emigrated from London, England, to Australia. As a young man he worked for a farm machinery maker and then went into business as a blacksmith, carpenter, and farmer in South Australia.

The plow that won Smith first prize at the 1876 agricultural show was very simple. However, it boosted wheat crops so much that people soon called the region the "breadbasket" of Australia.

Smith's eureka moment

Smith was farming land that had only recently been cleared of trees. They had such long roots that the stumps were impossible to dig up. Each time the plow hit a stump it jerked the horse, pulling it to a halt, or damaged the plow. This first happened to Smith when he was plowing in 1876. His plow struck a stump, snapping a bolt that held down the plow blade.

Though Smith's plow factory thrived and employed many workers, competitors copied his design. Fighting for credit as the plow's inventor, he apologized to a government committee for the crumpled state of his patent certificate: "I had to stow my papers in a box outside, and one rainy night a pig overturned it and made a bed out of the papers."

To Smith's amazement the horse did not stop. The plow's loose blade rode over the stump and continued plowing on the other side.

! EUREKA! Smith realized that a plow that was designed to jump over stumps would make plowing much quicker—and cut out the tough job of digging stumps from the soil.

What happened next?

Richard and his brother Clarence (1855–1901) got to work. By June 1876 they had built a plow and showed it at a local agricultural fair. Though it won first prize, local farmers did not like the idea of leaving stumps in the land. One shouted, "You're either a fool or a lunatic, Dick Smith. A plow's got to go in hard ground and stay unless you only want to tickle the soil."

In the end even the doubters bought Smith's plows. Before stump jumps farmers in South Australia plowed up just 5 sq. mi. (13 sq km) every year—an area small enough to walk around in two hours. After the invention they were turning scrublands into fields almost 30 times faster.

The first plow Smith sold, the Vixen, had three blades. Each one had a separate weight to force the blade firmly back into the soil after it "jumped" over a stump.

Richard Smith built a factory in Ardrossan, South Australia, to make his new type of plow—and later many other types of farm machinery. Today the factory is a museum and memorial to Smith's ingenuity.

POWERED FLIGHT

"Bird men" were jokes in the early 1900s, but this did not stop two American brothers from building giant kites and dreaming of flying in them. Orville and Wilbur Wright had trouble steering these first basic aircraft until Wilbur had a brilliant idea about how to control them.

But who were the Wright brothers?

Wilbur (1867–1912) and Orville (1871–1948) Wright ran a bicycle store in Dayton, Ohio. Neither finished high school, but their father, a bishop, encouraged them to study at home. The brothers combined scientific experiments and engineering to try to build a flying machine.

Lift, control, and power

The brothers began serious experiments in 1899 after reading about German glider pioneer Otto Lilienthal (1848–1896). He built and flew what we would now call hang gliders. Inspired, the brothers began building kites and gliders. They realized early on that to make an aircraft fly they would need to solve three problems: lift, to get it off the ground; control, so that they could go where they wanted to; and power, to move it forward. Before long they were building kites with plenty of lift. But control was more of a challenge. They watched pigeons in flight to see how they turned in the air and discussed the problem for long hours when business was slow at the bicycle store where they worked.

Wilbur's eureka moment

While selling a customer an inner tube for a bicycle tire Wilbur began tinkering with the box. He noticed that if he held one end and twisted the other, the normally flat surfaces of the box warped into gentle curves (see diagram above).

! **EUREKA!** Wilbur realized that if the box was the wing of their glider, air flowing over the curved surface would make it turn.

Wing warping!

It did not take them
long to put "wing warping"
into practice on the 5 ft.
(1.5m) kite they had built.
They tied strings to each
corner of its wings and
launched it in a strong
breeze. Making one string
tighter and the other looser
twisted the wings. Sure enough,
this steered the kite in the air—
just like a modern stunt kite. They
had solved the problem of control, but
the brothers still had a long way to go
before they could build an aircraft that
would fly. During the summer of 1900 they
made a 17-ft.-wingspan glider model. In the fall
they took it apart and shipped it to Kitty Hawk,
North Carolina, a beach with strong, steady winds.
Rebuilt, the glider was strong enough to ride on.
Later they flew it as a glider. In 1901 they returned
with a bigger glider. Back in Dayton they invented
the wind tunnel so that they could compare the
lifting ability of different wing shapes.

Flyer 1

They went back to Kitty Hawk again with
an improved glider in 1902 (above) and spent
the first half of the following year building a
powered craft (and incidentally inventing the
propeller). A week before Christmas that year
it flew. In an historic 59-second flight *Flyer 1*
(main image) was airborne for roughly the
length of a jumbo jet. Wilbur's (now patented)
wing-warp mechanism controlled its direction.

To make their 1903 aircraft fly the Wright brothers
needed an engine and propellers. When they found that
all the engines they could buy were too heavy, they had
a local mechanic build them a special lightweight motor.
Made mainly out of wood, canvas, and wire, the 1903
Flyer 1 had only enough power to lift the pilot.

THE HOVERCRAFT

Hoping to make a watercraft he built go faster, boat designer Christopher Cockerell realized it was the water that slowed it down. In 1955 he imagined that if he could wrap the hull in a cushion of air, it would almost skip along like a pebble spinning over the surface.

But who was Christopher Cockerell?

Extremely practical even as a boy, Christopher Cockerell (1910–1999) went to work for a British electronics company after finishing college. There he helped develop wartime radar sets and patented many other inventions. When his wife inherited some money, Cockerell started a boat-building business but soon returned to inventing.

Cockerell's eureka moment

To test his ideas about air-cushion vehicles in 1955 Cockerell experimented with jets of air. He tried making the jets narrower and wider to see what would provide the most lifting force.

Cockerell used an industrial fan for his experiments. He pointed it down onto the tray of a kitchen scale. Adding weights to the other side "weighed" the air pressure. He restricted the fan with empty coffee and cat food cans.

EUREKA! Cockerell discovered that making the jet narrower increased its power. And there was three times the pressure when air blew out of a narrow ring. He realized that a downward jet of air around the edge of a boat could make it hover just above the water!

On its first demonstration in Dover, England, the hovercraft traveled from the sea to the beach, but it was not a complete success. It threw up a huge cloud of spray and was safe only in calm weather.

Top secret!

Cockerell took his "hovercraft" to the British government. He told them it could travel fast over water, ice, marshes, or land. Unlike a plane or ship, it did not need a runway or a harbor. Military officials liked this. However, since it did not exactly belong in the army, the navy, or the air force, they declared the idea a secret . . . and then did nothing.

The first hovercraft had the "imaginative" name *SR–N1*. Here it is shown with a rubber skirt that enclosed the air cushion. This greatly increased the height at which it hovered so that small waves were no longer an obstacle.

Furious and short of money, the inventor sold his wife's jewelry to pay for hovercraft development, and in 1959 the first full-size hovercraft "flew" across the channel between England and France.

This cross section of a hovercraft shows how the vehicle's powerful engines draw in air and direct it down in order to provide lift. Jet engines at the rear drive it forward. Propellers, mounted on towers on the top, steer the hovercraft.

The United States Army experimented with military hovercraft during the Vietnam War (1954–1975), but the noise and spray they produced made them easy targets. The engines also sucked up seawater, which caused corrosion (rusting) and made them unreliable.

LENSES AND LIGHT

Playing in their father's store, an optician's children
lined up lenses—and invented the telescope. This lucky
accident was just one of several that changed the course
of optics—the science of light and lenses. Good luck and
sudden bright ideas played a part in the invention
of photography and instant pictures as well.

THE TELESCOPE

It may have been a children's game that gave a humble optician the idea of lining up two lenses to magnify distant things. Hans Lippershey tried to keep this 1608 invention a secret, but news of his "magic tube" spread quickly. In Italy a brilliant young scientist used one to shake up our understanding of the universe and our place in it.

To enlarge distant objects Lippershey's young children had to choose the right lenses and hold them the correct distance apart. It was fortunate that the combination of the two lenses worked.

But who was Hans Lippershey?

We do not know much about the inventor of the telescope. Even his name is uncertain: was it Hans Lippershey, Jan Lippersheim, or Hans Lippersheim? He was born around 1570 in Wesel, Germany, and by 1608 he was living and working as an optician in Middelburg in the Netherlands. His store was located conveniently close to the glass factory in the town.

Lippershey's eureka moment

Hans Lippershey's two children were playing with a few eyeglass lenses in the optician's store. Holding them up in a straight line and looking through both, they could see an enlarged image of storks nesting on a distant steeple.

EUREKA! Their father instantly saw the possibilities of this device, and Lippershey placed the lenses into a tube to produce what he called a "looker."

Lippershey's children made a lucky choice, for on their own neither of the two lenses they picked up was interesting. One was a weak magnifying glass, and the other made things look smaller.

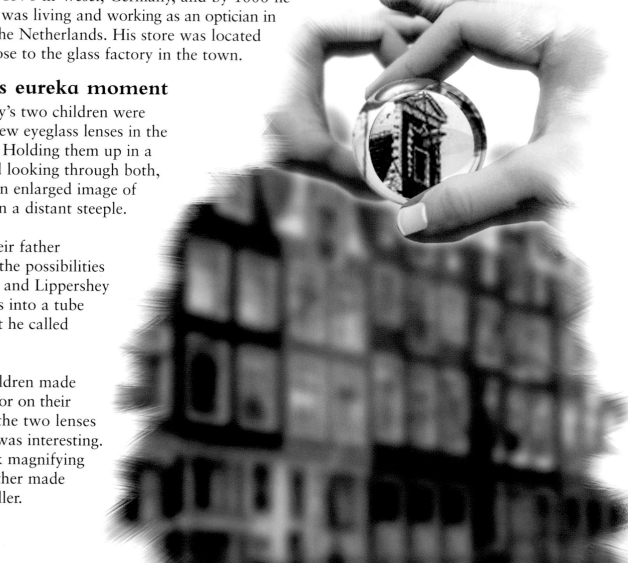

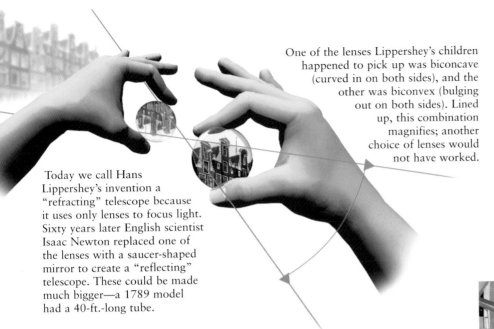

One of the lenses Lippershey's children happened to pick up was biconcave (curved in on both sides), and the other was biconvex (bulging out on both sides). Lined up, this combination magnifies; another choice of lenses would not have worked.

Today we call Hans Lippershey's invention a "refracting" telescope because it uses only lenses to focus light. Sixty years later English scientist Isaac Newton replaced one of the lenses with a saucer-shaped mirror to create a "reflecting" telescope. These could be made much bigger—a 1789 model had a 40-ft.-long tube.

Keeping secrets

There are several other versions of this story; four hundred years later it is hard to separate fact from fiction. However, we can be sure about what followed. The optician took his invention to the regional council, hoping to protect it with a patent. The council sent him to the Dutch commander-in-chief, who immediately saw how the telescope could be used in warfare. He sent the optician away with a sizable reward, an order for three more telescopes . . . and demanded that he tell no one about the invention. Despite this warning, the telescope was not kept a secret for long. Nine months later Italian scientist Galileo Galilei heard a rumor about a device made from tubes and lenses that made faraway objects appear closer.

Earth's atmosphere blocks much of the light from distant stars. So instead some powerful telescopes, such as *The Very Large Array* (below) in New Mexico, use radio waves, focusing them with curved reflectors like television satellite dishes.

Galileo's telescope

After just 24 hours of frantic experiments Galileo had produced a working telescope, and within weeks he had greatly improved the instrument. Galileo's telescopes were eight times more powerful than Hans Lippershey's. They were good enough to impress the doge (duke) of Venice.

Telescopes can focus light using mirrors, which can be made bigger than lenses, creating a brighter picture.

Important discoveries

Galileo (who also devised the pendulum clock, see pages 12–13) used the telescope to make startling astronomical observations. Perhaps the most important of these were of the moons of Jupiter. By watching how they moved around the planet Galileo was able to prove that the center of the universe was the Sun, not Earth, as many people believed at the time.

PHOTOGRAPHY

When French scene painter Louis Daguerre first showed off his newly invented photography process in 1839, the people of Paris, France, were astonished. Each picture looked like a mirror—a mirror that "remembered" what it had reflected. Even more astonishing was the story of how a lucky discovery had helped Daguerre perfect the process.

New lenses that let in 16 times as much light cut the time taken to make a photograph to under one minute. This made portraits possible—as long as the subject's head was held still in a clamp! Daguerre used his wife as a model for this portrait.

But who was Louis Daguerre?

Artistic and agile, Louis Daguerre (1787–1851) drew pictures and walked tightropes with equal ability. He became a scene painter at the opera, but his goal was to make pictures paint themselves. He tinkered with light, lenses, and chemicals and also teamed up with another experimenter, Nicéphore Niepce (1765–1833). The two had still not found a practical process by the time Niepce died.

Daguerre's eureka moment

Daguerre discovered that iodine vapor made a shiny silver plate sensitive to light. A very faint picture formed on the plate if he exposed it in a camera. Nothing made the picture less faint—until he left a plate inside a cabinet he used to store chemicals. In the morning there was a clear image on it! A chemical in the cupboard was making the picture appear, but which chemical was it? Daguerre put a plate in the cupboard night after night, removing one chemical at a time. Even with the cupboard empty, the trick still worked. Then Daguerre noticed that the cupboard was not completely empty. In the bottom were some tiny drops of mercury left by a broken thermometer.

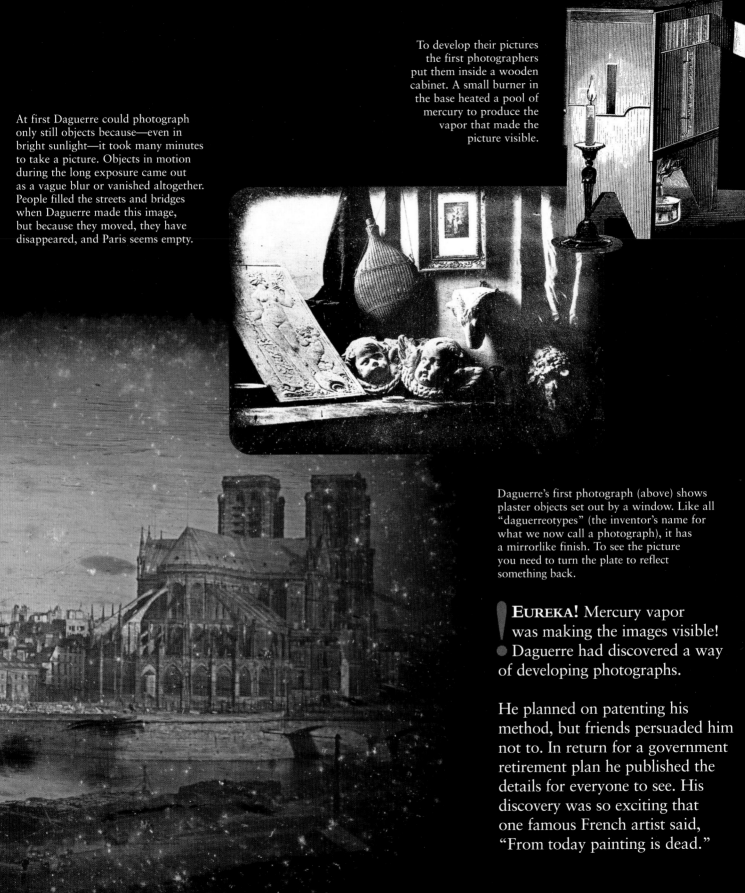

At first Daguerre could photograph only still objects because—even in bright sunlight—it took many minutes to take a picture. Objects in motion during the long exposure came out as a vague blur or vanished altogether. People filled the streets and bridges when Daguerre made this image, but because they moved, they have disappeared, and Paris seems empty.

To develop their pictures the first photographers put them inside a wooden cabinet. A small burner in the base heated a pool of mercury to produce the vapor that made the picture visible.

Daguerre's first photograph (above) shows plaster objects set out by a window. Like all "daguerreotypes" (the inventor's name for what we now call a photograph), it has a mirrorlike finish. To see the picture you need to turn the plate to reflect something back.

EUREKA! Mercury vapor was making the images visible! Daguerre had discovered a way of developing photographs.

He planned on patenting his method, but friends persuaded him not to. In return for a government retirement plan he published the details for everyone to see. His discovery was so exciting that one famous French artist said, "From today painting is dead."

POLAROID

When Edwin Land took a picture of his three-year-old daughter on vacation in 1943, her impatience sparked the American's inventive spirit. It took Land three years to satisfy his daughter's curiosity, but her simple question helped make him one of America's most admired—and richest—men.

But who was Edwin Land?

Physicist Edwin Land (1909–1991) dropped out of college to make the reflection-killing material he later called Polaroid—and also because he was smarter than many of his teachers! Restlessly creative, he patented more inventions than anyone except Thomas Edison (see pages 68–69).

The first instant photos now seem very basic, as this snapshot of Land shows. They had wavy edges and were brown and white at a time when color pictures were becoming popular. However, the novelty of instantly seeing the picture definitely made up for these drawbacks.

Land's Polaroid corporation became one of the most successful companies in the United States. Besides instant cameras, they also made weapon parts for the U.S. Army and helped build spy planes.

Land's eureka moment

"Why can't I see it now?" Land's daughter Jennifer asked as soon as the shutter had clicked. "Yes . . . " he thought, "Why shouldn't she see it now?"

EUREKA! If Land could make a camera that developed the pictures as well as taking them, everybody would want one— at heart even adults are as impatient as a three-year-old child to see themselves on film.

Not all of Land's ideas were winners— "instant movies" flopped. They needed a projector and ran for only three minutes. They could not compete with home videos, which played for one hour on a TV set.

You had to load two rolls of film to use Land's 1946 camera (above). After taking the picture pulling a tab brought both rolls together and burst a bag of chemicals between them. You peeled the film apart to see the finished picture. With Polaroid "One Step" film, introduced in 1972, the picture appeared while you watched.

Land joked later that he solved all of the technical problems of instant photography that same afternoon, " . . . except for the ones it took the next 19 years to solve." He meant that he had figured out the basic science in hours, but it took much longer to make a working camera. Land's first Polaroid camera, introduced in 1946, was not exactly instant. It took one minute to make brown-and-white pictures. He gradually improved the process, making the pictures true black-and-white and reducing developing time to ten seconds. In 1972 he launched color pictures that developed instantly.

Today's instant cameras (right) are sleek, smooth, and shiny. Nevertheless there is still a thrill in watching them produce a shiny little picture that you can slip into a frame one or two minutes after saying "Cheese."

ELECTRICITY

In the ancient world people knew about electricity:
2,600 years ago the Greeks rubbed amber together
to make sparks. But it was not until the 1600s
that scientists began to truly study electricity—
with the aid of some sparks of inspiration.
Eureka moments helped bring electric power and
convenience into our homes in the 1900s as well.

THE LIGHTNING CONDUCTOR

ZZZZAP! With a clap of thunder, a bolt of lightning hits a tall building. But it took a daring experiment in the 1750s by American statesman Benjamin Franklin to prove that lightning is a type of electricity and then to invent protection against it.

This painting of Franklin flying his kite with a key tied to the string made the experiment famous. However, experts argue about whether Franklin was the first or whether he was repeating experiments done by European scientists.

But who was Benjamin Franklin?

Though he was also a writer and printer, Benjamin Franklin (1706–1790) is best known as an American politician. He did a lot to help his country break free from British rule during the Revolutionary War (1775–1783). He was a scientist and inventor, too, and in 1752 he was fascinated with newly discovered electricity.

A special type of kite

Franklin was fairly sure that thunderstorms were electric, so he devised a simple but daring experiment. It was very dangerous—do not try to repeat it yourself! Franklin's experiment was to fly a special type of kite in a storm. He wanted to see if electricity from the thunderstorm would flow down the kite string.

Though they protect the building they are attached to, lightning conductors can themselves be damaged by lightning strikes. One thunderbolt was powerful enough to melt the tip of this lightning conductor so that it flopped over on one side.

Safety silk

The kite had a sharp, pointed wire attached to it to attract electricity. It also had a safety device—a silk ribbon tied to the end of the string. Electricity does not flow through silk. So by holding the ribbon and not the string Franklin protected himself from a shock if lightning struck. As the kite rose into the clouds lightning struck, and electricity traveled down the string. Sparks flew from the key—just as Franklin had predicted!

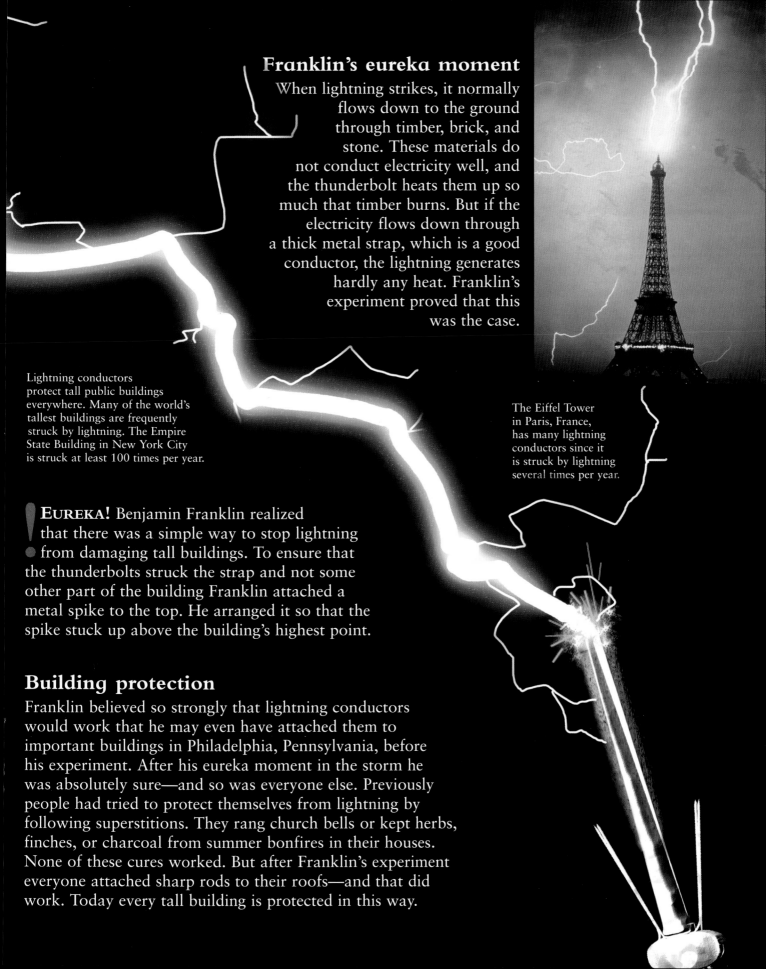

Franklin's eureka moment

When lightning strikes, it normally flows down to the ground through timber, brick, and stone. These materials do not conduct electricity well, and the thunderbolt heats them up so much that timber burns. But if the electricity flows down through a thick metal strap, which is a good conductor, the lightning generates hardly any heat. Franklin's experiment proved that this was the case.

Lightning conductors protect tall public buildings everywhere. Many of the world's tallest buildings are frequently struck by lightning. The Empire State Building in New York City is struck at least 100 times per year.

The Eiffel Tower in Paris, France, has many lightning conductors since it is struck by lightning several times per year.

EUREKA! Benjamin Franklin realized that there was a simple way to stop lightning from damaging tall buildings. To ensure that the thunderbolts struck the strap and not some other part of the building Franklin attached a metal spike to the top. He arranged it so that the spike stuck up above the building's highest point.

Building protection

Franklin believed so strongly that lightning conductors would work that he may even have attached them to important buildings in Philadelphia, Pennsylvania, before his experiment. After his eureka moment in the storm he was absolutely sure—and so was everyone else. Previously people had tried to protect themselves from lightning by following superstitions. They rang church bells or kept herbs, finches, or charcoal from summer bonfires in their houses. None of these cures worked. But after Franklin's experiment everyone attached sharp rods to their roofs—and that did work. Today every tall building is protected in this way.

THE ELECTRICAL BATTERY

While cutting up frogs on a stormy day in the late 1700s Luigi Galvani noticed that the legs twitched if he jabbed them with his sharp knife. Galvani thought lightning from the storm might be causing the movement. He did not fully understand what he had discovered, but his experiments led to the electrical battery.

Volta found that producing more electricity was as simple as adding an extra cell—a "sandwich" of soggy cardboard and metal disks—to his pile. Today such an arrangement of cells connected together is still called a *pile* in the French language. In English we call it a battery.

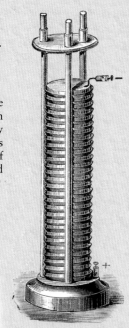

But who was Luigi Galvani?

Italian medical student Luigi Galvani (1737–1798) became interested in anatomy and physiology—the structure of animals and how their bodies work. It was this interest that led him, almost 25 years later, to wire a frog's legs in an electrical circuit.

Frog power

When Galvani hung the frog's legs on a rack outside his window to dry, he saw them twitch in thundery weather. But to his surprise the legs moved even on clear days.

Galvani's eureka moment

Galvani knew about Benjamin Franklin's experiments with lightning (see pages 62–63), and he was sure that electricity was causing the movement.

❗ EUREKA! Since the legs twitched when there was no thunder in the air Galvani thought that the animal's muscles and nerves must have been generating power.

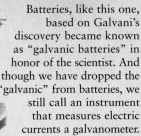

Batteries, like this one, based on Galvani's discovery became known as "galvanic batteries" in honor of the scientist. And though we have dropped the "galvanic" from batteries, we still call an instrument that measures electric currents a galvanometer.

Animal battery

He was half right. It was true that electricity was causing the muscles to move. But the power did not come from the frog itself. In fact, Galvani had invented a simple electrical cell. On his drying rack the legs touched two different metals—brass and iron. These have different abilities to attract electrons (tiny particles that flow in an electric circuit). Fluid in the frog's body allowed the electrons to flow as an electric current, and it was this current that caused the muscular twitches.

Galvani got it wrong

Physics professor Alessandro Volta (1745–1827) read Galvani's essay on the subject of electricity, *Commentary on the Effect of Electricity on Muscular Motion*. Volta was sure Galvani was wrong, so he tried repeating the experiments.

Volta became famous for his battery. In 1801 he showed it to French ruler Napoleon Bonaparte (1769–1821), who made him a count and a senator. Volta's name lives on in the volt— the unit of electric force.

Building a "pile"

Volta experimented with many animals and metals and found that some pairs of metals worked better than others. Finally he stacked up zinc and silver plates, slipping cardboard pads soaked in salty water in between them. This produced much more power than a single cell (pair of plates). Between them, Galvani and Volta had invented the battery.

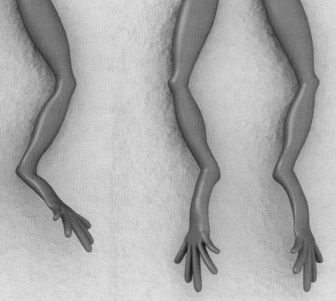

Tiny electric currents flowing in the nerves of living animals make their muscles move. Even after death the muscles react to electricity, as Galvani discovered. But what he did not realize was that the source of the power was not the animal itself but the two metals touching it.

THE TELEPHONE

Italian–American theater engineer Antonio Meucci thought electricity might cure migraines, so he wired a "patient" to a battery. But it was Meucci who got a shock when sound traveled around his circuit! He called his 1849 invention the "speaking telegraph." We would later call it a telephone.

Meucci made many different telephones during his experiments. He was using this one, made from carved wood, around 1858, nine years before Bell's patent. A disk of paper stretched across the opening in the wide wooden base moved a coil of wire inside.

But who was Antonio Meucci?

Antonio Meucci (1808–1896) emigrated from Italy to Cuba in 1835. There he set up the country's first metal-coating factory and dabbled in the fashionable trend of treating the sick with electricity.

Ouch!

Meucci put a metal plate in a migraine sufferer's mouth and connected the plate to a battery. Before switching on the current Meucci put a similar plate in his own mouth and adjusted the power to a comfortable level. Then he flipped on the switch.

Bell (right) perhaps copied Meucci's invention when the two worked together in a shared laboratory. Later workers at Bell's company probably bribed officials in the U.S. patent office to destroy documents that proved Meucci's telephone was the first. Bell grew rich from his stolen invention and hired leading lawyers to fight Meucci (left) when the inventor tried to challenge his claim.

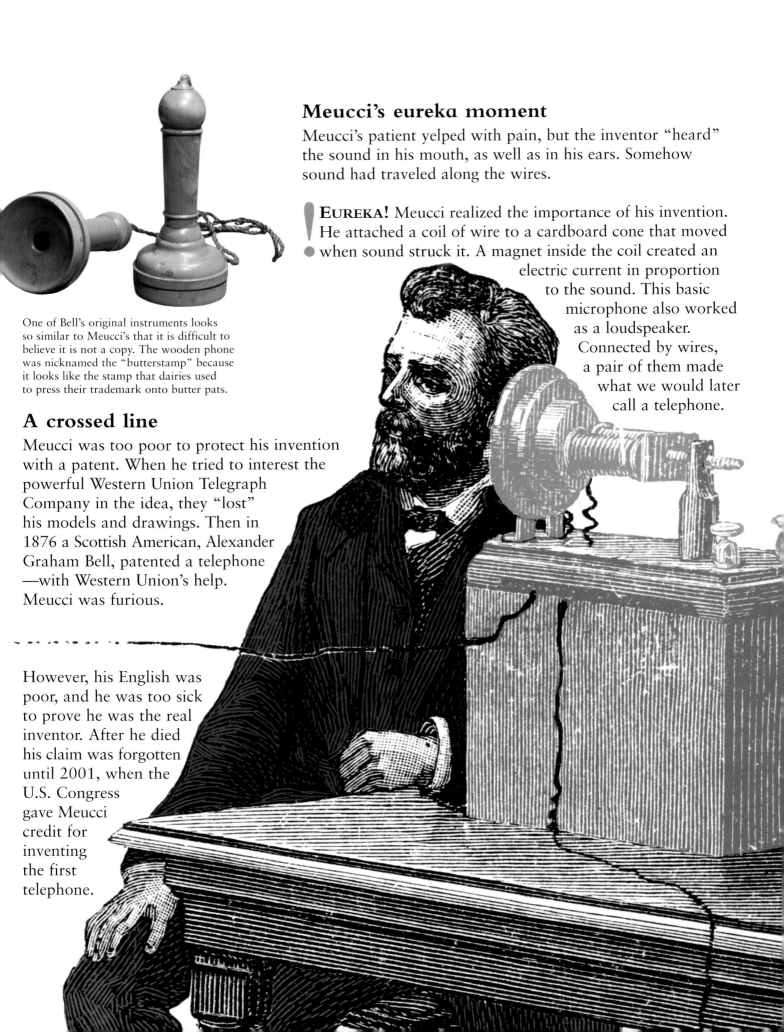

Meucci's eureka moment

Meucci's patient yelped with pain, but the inventor "heard" the sound in his mouth, as well as in his ears. Somehow sound had traveled along the wires.

! EUREKA! Meucci realized the importance of his invention. He attached a coil of wire to a cardboard cone that moved when sound struck it. A magnet inside the coil created an electric current in proportion to the sound. This basic microphone also worked as a loudspeaker. Connected by wires, a pair of them made what we would later call a telephone.

One of Bell's original instruments looks so similar to Meucci's that it is difficult to believe it is not a copy. The wooden phone was nicknamed the "butterstamp" because it looks like the stamp that dairies used to press their trademark onto butter pats.

A crossed line

Meucci was too poor to protect his invention with a patent. When he tried to interest the powerful Western Union Telegraph Company in the idea, they "lost" his models and drawings. Then in 1876 a Scottish American, Alexander Graham Bell, patented a telephone —with Western Union's help. Meucci was furious.

However, his English was poor, and he was too sick to prove he was the real inventor. After he died his claim was forgotten until 2001, when the U.S. Congress gave Meucci credit for inventing the first telephone.

THE LIGHTBULB

When people called American inventor Thomas Edison a genius, he had a slick reply: "Genius is one percent inspiration . . . and 99 percent perspiration." He certainly sweated for months to create his 1880 lightbulb, but he also had a eureka moment that helped him make it work.

When Edison's lightbulb experiments dragged on longer than expected, he said, "I have not failed. I have just found 10,000 ways that will not work."

But who was Thomas Edison?

Bored by school, Thomas Alva Edison (1847–1931) stormed out when a teacher insulted him. Studying science at home, he once wired two cats together, hoping to see sparks fly when he stroked them. Edison got a job operating the telegraph (the predecessor of the telephone) and made a fortune inventing ways to speed up the messages it carried.

Subdividing the electric light

When Edison was a boy, electric lamps already glowed brightly—too brightly! Powerful enough for a street, they were much too bright for a room. Inventors called the challenge of lighting homes "subdividing" the electric light—into smaller, less blinding parts. Edison started looking for a solution in 1878. He thought it would take six weeks. However, he soon had problems with the glowing filament (metal wire) inside the glass bulbs. Whatever he made it from the bulbs burned out too soon. After one year of experiments he had made little progress.

Edison's eureka moment

Working late one night, Edison idly fiddled with a piece of carbon cake—a mixture of soot and sticky tar. Rolling it between his fingers, he made it into a thin sausage shape.

EUREKA! Suddenly it struck Edison that this might work better as a filament than anything he had tried before.

Edison and his engineers developed the lightbulb at a laboratory built specifically for them in Menlo Park, New Jersey. It was the first research laboratory ever created, and it is now preserved as a museum.

Until Edison developed lightbulbs the only electric lights were arc lamps, which created an electric spark between a pair of pencil-sized sticks of carbon. Bright enough to light a circus tent, they were much too powerful for homes.

What happened next?

Edison relied on a team of engineers to make his good ideas work. One of them, Francis Upton (1852–1921), helped Edison turn his carbon cake roll into a filament. By October 1879 they had made a lamp that glowed for 40 hours, but it was still not good enough. Nobody wanted a bulb that burned out in one week.

But Edison was not beaten. By spring he had built not only long-lasting lamps but wires, switches, and a generator and had installed them on a ship. House and office lights soon followed. Edison's "six-week" problem had taken him two years to solve!

THE TELEPHONE EXCHANGE

The first telephones had no dials or buttons. To call a friend you asked an operator for the number you wanted. She used a cable to link your telephone line to your friend's. The system worked well as long as there were not many phones and everyone knew which number they wanted. But as undertaker Almon Strowger found out in 1888, operators sometimes had their own ideas about who you wanted to call . . .

But who was Almon Strowger?

After graduating from college Almon Strowger (1839–1902) fought in the Civil War. He then worked as a schoolteacher before setting up an undertaker's business in Kansas City, Kansas, in 1886.

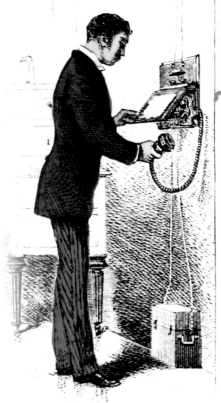

Strowger's eureka moment

Strowger had become suspicious when his telephone stopped ringing. His anxiety grew when he found out that another funeral parlor was doing much better than his own. After investigating the situation he discovered that his rival was dating the telephone operator. When people called the exchange and asked her for an undertaker, she was connecting them to her boyfriend!

EUREKA! Strowger realized that if he devised an automatic switch, he could remove the need for a telephone operator. Then people who needed an undertaker could call him directly—and his business would flourish again.

With some improvements Almon Strowger's automatic switches were installed by the million. They remained the main way of connecting calls for over 70 years. The telephones were improved too— dials soon replaced the push buttons, which were awkward to use and often dialed wrong numbers.

The telephone service began when women were fighting for equal rights. A telephone operator's job was "respectable" at a time when there were few opportunities for women to work. As the telephone network grew, however, no matter how many women exchanges employed, they could not keep up with the calls. Strowger's invention came just in time to prevent total chaos.

Collar-box switch

Strowger got to work making a switch using electromagnets and pins pushed into a round cardboard box that used to contain shirt collars. By 1891 he had devised a switch that worked, and he protected it with a patent. He installed his first automatic exchange in La Porte, Indiana, the following year.

Strowger's telephones worked with push buttons. To dial "215" you pressed the first button twice, the second button once, and the third button five times. Each press moved a switch at the exchange, connecting the call.

RADIO

Some of the world's greatest scientists studied radio waves, but it was an unknown 20-year-old Italian who sent the first radio messages. In 1894 Guglielmo Marconi began experimenting with a basic transmitter that used sparks of electricity to create radio waves. A simple receiver picked up the waves on the other side of the room, so he tried moving it much farther away . . .

Marconi's broadcast across the Atlantic Ocean was a huge risk. He had to build 20 antennas, each 200 ft. tall, in Poldhu, England, and Cape Cod, Newfoundland. The experiment cost $75,000—the equivalent of almost $5 million in today's money. Marconi worried that Earth's curvature would block out the broadcast, but on December 12, 1901 his apparatus in Newfoundland received three short signals—the Morse code signal for the letter "S." He had done it!

But who was Guglielmo Marconi?

Guglielmo Marconi (1874–1937) failed the entrance exams at Bologna University in Italy, but his father managed to sneak him into the lectures and labs. After learning about experiments with radio he set up a workshop at home in an attic room once used for breeding silkworms.

Marconi received his historic signal in a station set up just below the Cabot Tower in Cape Cod, Newfoundland. He chose this spot because nowhere in North America is closer to Europe and also because an antenna located on the high cliffs there would get much better reception than one on low ground.

Marconi's eureka moment

Marconi did not actually invent anything new. Radio waves had already been discovered; the designs of his transmitter and receiver were copied from those of other scientists. But the young Italian thought of a new use for radio waves. He realized that he could use them to send messages without wires. Nobody before him had thought about doing this.

Eureka! Marconi sent his brother outside into the yard with the receiver. Alfonso (1865–1936) walked away from the house, waving a white handkerchief to show when he received a broadcast. By 1895 Alfonso carried the receiver into the next valley! His signal—a blast from a hunting rifle—proved that even a hill could not stop radio waves from traveling.

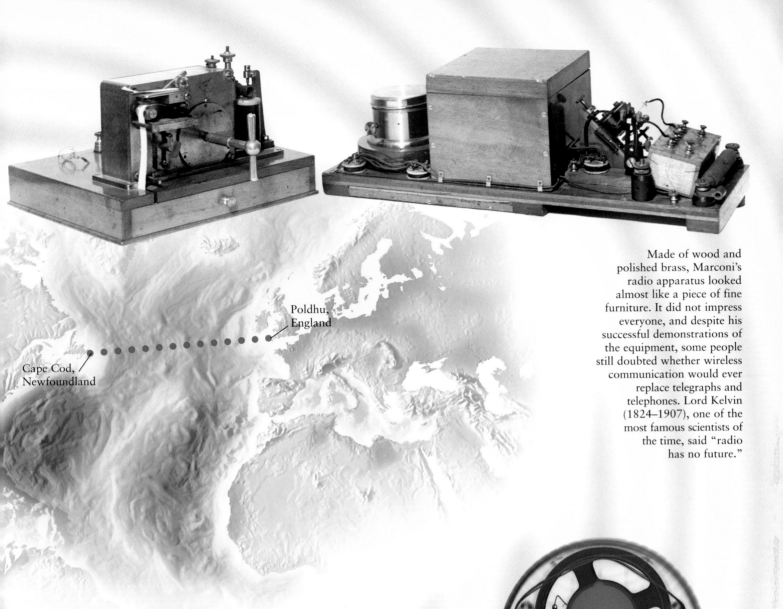

Made of wood and polished brass, Marconi's radio apparatus looked almost like a piece of fine furniture. It did not impress everyone, and despite his successful demonstrations of the equipment, some people still doubted whether wireless communication would ever replace telegraphs and telephones. Lord Kelvin (1824–1907), one of the most famous scientists of the time, said "radio has no future."

Poldhu, England

Cape Cod, Newfoundland

Waves across the world

Convinced that his idea was a breakthrough in communication, Marconi approached the Italian Post Office. The stuffy government officials there were not interested in "wireless" communication. But once again his family helped him out. His Irish-Scottish mother brought him to Great Britain, where one of his cousins introduced him to William Preece (1834–1913), the head engineer at the British Post Office. With Preece's help, Marconi improved his apparatus so that his broadcasts reached across London, England, and then across the English Channel. In an historic moment in 1901 Marconi broadcast a faint radio signal across the Atlantic. The world suddenly seemed to be a much smaller place!

Marconi made all of our modern uses for radio possible, from tiny pocket receivers like this one to portable telephones and wireless computer networks.

TELEVISION

When Scottish inventor John Logie Baird gazed at the first television pictures in 1926, he experienced an unforgettable eureka moment. Though his mechanical television system was soon overtaken by electronic competitors, it was Baird who truly started the television industry. Because of Baird's infectious enthusiasm, television broadcasts began—even though only 30 people had television sets to watch the blurred and flickering pictures.

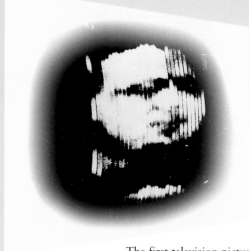

The first television pictures were very poor quality because they were made up of just 30 scan lines. Though modern TV sets still scan the screen in a similar way, they use over 600 lines, so pictures are 20 times clearer.

But who was Baird?

While his friends at school were making telephones with tin cans and string John Logie Baird (1888–1946) wired his neighborhood with real telephones, complete with an exchange. Though his teachers called him "slow" and "timid," Baird managed to get accepted at Glasgow University in Scotland to study electrical engineering.

Baird had a knack for both amazing and off-the-wall publicity stunts. As part of his campaign to get his TV system adopted in 1926 he gave this first experimental transmitter to the Science Museum in London, England. Parts of it turned out to be bogus.

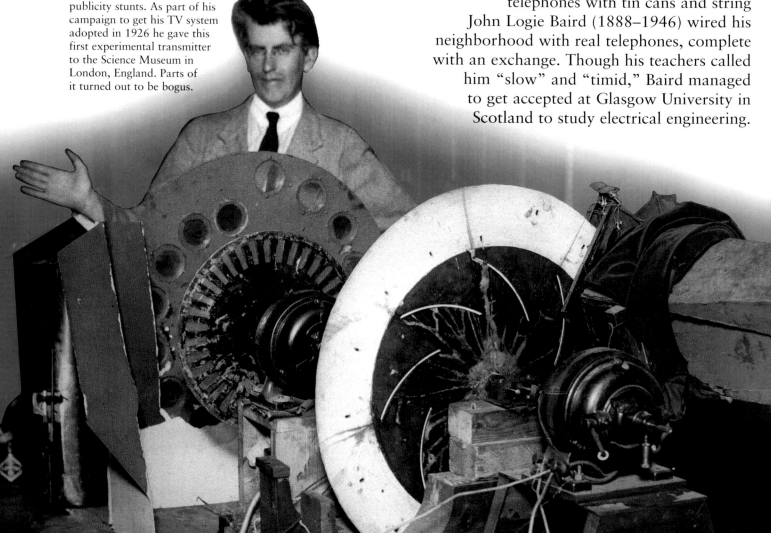

Baird's eureka moment

Ambitious and eccentric, Baird tried his hand at making artificial diamonds and tropical fruit jams. When these ventures failed, he turned to the idea of broadcasting moving pictures by radio. He made money during the day and did research at night in a makeshift laboratory in London, England. His television camera was a jumble of lenses, spinning cardboard disks, and electric motors pointed at the head of a mannequin named Stooky Bill. Amazingly, it worked.

! EUREKA! According to Baird, "The image of the mannequin's head formed itself on the screen with what appeared to me an almost unbelievable clarity."

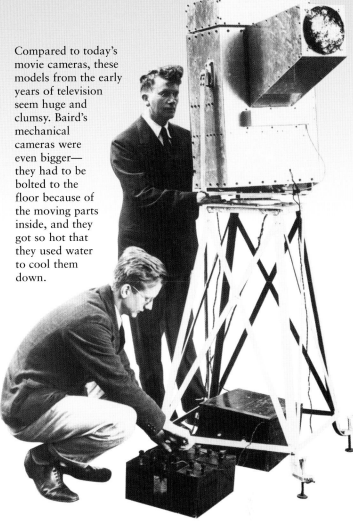

Compared to today's movie cameras, these models from the early years of television seem huge and clumsy. Baird's mechanical cameras were even bigger— they had to be bolted to the floor because of the moving parts inside, and they got so hot that they used water to cool them down.

A large wooden box held the whirling disk that generated the picture on Baird's first TV sets. The screen, which was roughly the size of a playing card, was inside the square black tube on the top right. These receivers were so simple that some viewers built their own.

Total conviction

Not everyone agreed with Baird. Most people only saw a flickering blur, but Baird was convinced that his system would work. Through smart publicity, determination, and sheer stubbornness he managed to get the BBC (British Broadcasting Corporation) to start experimental TV programs.

But Baird's success did not last long. When the BBC started a full TV service in 1937, they decided that whirling disks could not produce pictures that were good enough. They dropped Baird's system and chose all-electronic television instead. Baird's business collapsed, and he died nine years later a bitter and disappointed man.

PATIENCE AND PLANNING

If we relied on eureka moments to inspire all science
and inventions, we would live in a primitive world
without any modern conveniences. Such strokes of
genius are rare, and in these last few stories you
will see how determination and hard work are
more reliable ways to succeed.

THE "REAL" MCCOY

Eureka moments help us remember incredible inventors, but for every scientist whose work made them famous many more were overlooked. The history of technology was mainly written by white men who did not value the contributions of female and black inventors. Most of these people are forgotten, or their work is claimed by other, more famous, inventors. Elijah McCoy is one of the few who received full credit for his achievement in 1872.

But who was Elijah McCoy?

The son of escaped Kentucky slaves, Elijah McCoy (1843–1929) was brought up in Canada. He was a curious child and was handy at fixing things, so his parents sent him to Scotland to study engineering. When he returned, the fact that he was black kept him from getting work as an engineer. He had to take up a job shoveling coal and oiling locomotives.

McCoy's original automatic lubricator was like a cup of oil with a valve powered by steam. The harder the engine worked, the more the steam pressure rose—and the faster the oil flowed out. McCoy designed this improved lubricator in 1882, ten years after his first patent.

McCoy's invention

Steam engines needed constant lubrication (oiling) to keep them running. In the time McCoy spent squirting an oil can he wondered if he could make the train oil itself. He scraped together enough money to build a workshop and toiled for two years to solve the problem. By 1872 he had invented an automatic lubricator, and he protected it with a patent. Other engineers quickly realized the advantages of McCoy's new device and installed it on their trains. When inferior copies became a problem, people buying lubricators asked, "Is this the 'real' McCoy?"—and the inventor's name became another word for "quality."

American railroads were booming when McCoy was working as a stoker and part-time inventor. A railroad connected the east and west coasts only three years before his first patent. Lubrication was a major problem. Engines often overheated from a lack of oil, leading to delays.

SOUND RECORDING

American inventor Thomas Edison cleverly encouraged the idea that he was a creative genius. When he invented a way of recording sound in 1877, he spread a story that he had then worked for four days without sleep to perfect the phonograph. In reality it was four months before he even realized the value of what he had discovered.

A distinct sound

In the summer of 1877 Thomas Edison (see pages 68–69) was trying to store and amplify signals from the newly invented telephone. He had built a device that used a needle to scratch sound waves into a moving strip of wax paper. He shouted "Hello" into it and was surprised to discover that when he pulled the paper strip through the machine again, he heard a distinct sound, which a strong imagination could have translated into the original "Hello."

At the time Edison was so absorbed with his telephone amplifier, which he called a phonograph from the Greek words for "sound" and "writing." He realized much later on that he could use the machine to play back speech. In November 1877 he began working on adapting his phonograph for this new purpose.

Edison's competitors improved on the phonograph by replacing the tinfoil with wax cylinders, which produced a better sound quality and were more durable. The new machines, called graphophones, were widely used as office dictating machines and to preserve historic sounds—such as the language of the Blackfoot tribe.

Phonograph sales began in 1878, sparking a craze for the machines. People lined up to visit "phonograph parlors" just to hear short pieces of music or a few jokes by a popular comedian. However, novelty was not enough to make up for the poor sound quality and other drawbacks. After one year the public lost interest in what Edison himself described as "a mere toy."

Edison's first phonograph was very basic and needed very careful adjustment to produce any sound at all.

Building the recorder

Edison gave his engineer a drawing, telling him, "The machine must talk." He later commented, "I did not have much faith that it would work." Neither did any of his workers—they all bet cigars on the failure of the project.

When the machine was completed, everyone gathered around. Edison wrapped a sheet of tinfoil around the cylinder and recited "Mary had a little lamb" into the mouthpiece. After rewinding the tape the machine played back the nursery rhyme in Edison's distinctive voice. He later said: "I was never so taken aback in my life. I was always afraid of things that work the first time." On December 6, 1877 Edison demonstrated the phonograph at the offices of *Scientific American* magazine.

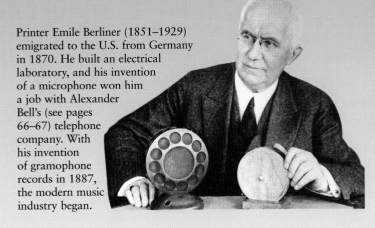

Printer Emile Berliner (1851–1929) emigrated to the U.S. from Germany in 1870. He built an electrical laboratory, and his invention of a microphone won him a job with Alexander Bell's (see pages 66–67) telephone company. With his invention of gramophone records in 1887, the modern music industry began.

Disks replace cyclinders

The phonograph made Edison famous, but it was far from perfect. Recordings played for only one minute and quickly wore out. But in 1888 more durable disks replaced the cylinders, and the gramophone that played them survived almost unchanged until the introduction of CDs almost one hundred years later.

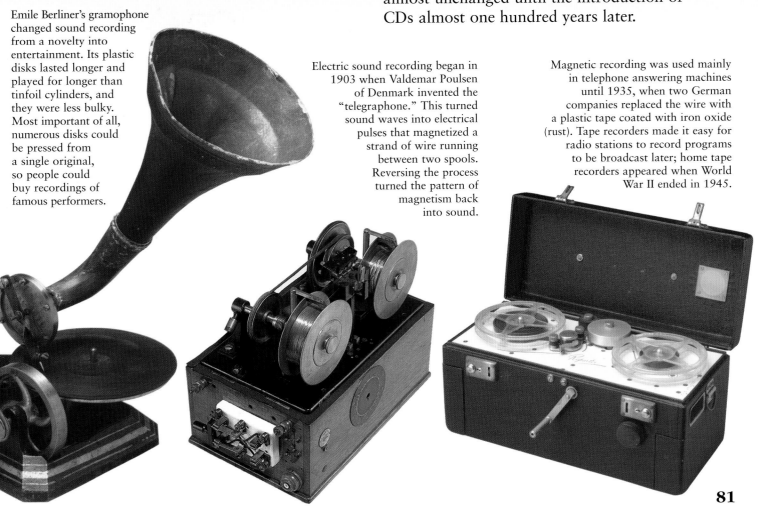

Emile Berliner's gramophone changed sound recording from a novelty into entertainment. Its plastic disks lasted longer and played for longer than tinfoil cylinders, and they were less bulky. Most important of all, numerous disks could be pressed from a single original, so people could buy recordings of famous performers.

Electric sound recording began in 1903 when Valdemar Poulsen of Denmark invented the "telegraphone." This turned sound waves into electrical pulses that magnetized a strand of wire running between two spools. Reversing the process turned the pattern of magnetism back into sound.

Magnetic recording was used mainly in telephone answering machines until 1935, when two German companies replaced the wire with a plastic tape coated with iron oxide (rust). Tape recorders made it easy for radio stations to record programs to be broadcast later; home tape recorders appeared when World War II ended in 1945.

THE SAFETY BICYCLE

Over one hundred years ago John Starley introduced the first modern bicycle. It was more than just sudden inspiration that made his 1885 "Rover" model so popular. Starley succeeded because he brought together the spokes, tires, and chains that other inventors had perfected.

Starley's safety bicycles were safer because they had smaller wheels. Starley's first two bicycles were not a huge success, but his third, built in 1885, was a special design. Its new diamond-shaped frame made it strong, light, and safe.

But who was John Starley?

The son of a gardener in London, England, John Kemp Starley (1854–1901) moved north to Coventry, England, when he was 18 to work at his uncle James Starley's sewing machine business. James Starley patented the first tricycle four years later. John Starley helped him build tricycles, but in 1877 he left to start his own bicycle business.

Bicycles were not the result of one single idea. It took a series of gradual improvements to produce a machine that was practical, safe, and comfortable. In 1817 German Karl Drais (1785–1851) invented the "running machine"—a two-wheeled hobbyhorse (below) pushed forward with the feet.

Dangerous beginnings

Scotsman Kirkpatrick Macmillan invented the bicycle in 1839. He based it on earlier "hobbyhorses," which riders pushed along with their feet. However, Macmillan's bicycle weighed almost 55 lbs. (25kg) and was uncomfortable to ride.

Other inventors improved on Macmillan's clumsy design, but bicycles were still dangerous machines when John Starley became interested in them. The pedals that pushed them forward were attached to the front wheels. To make the bicycle go fast enough the front wheel had to be huge.

Scottish blacksmith Kirkpatrick Macmillan (1810–1878) and others added pedals to the front wheel, creating new bicycles called "velocipedes" (below).

Spokes, chains, and tires

John Starley invented the diamond frame—not the bicycle itself. However, in his Rover safety bicycle he brought together many good ideas for the first time.

Starley's 1885 bicycle did not only rely on the innovative diamond frame—the wheels also had special spokes. Spokes themselves were nothing new. They were invented 36 years earlier to make the landing wheels of a glider lighter. But Starley added a clever twist. He attached alternate spokes to the left and right sides of the axle. If a wheel buckled, it could be straightened by tightening or loosening the spokes. Starley made his bicycle go fast by attaching a big gearwheel to the pedals. A chain wrapped around it powered a small gear on the rear wheel. This was not Starley's idea either. Harry Lawson (1852–1925), the manager of a bicycle company in Coventry, had made a chain-driven bicycle in 1879.

The final improvement that ensured the success of Starley's design were air-filled tires, introduced in 1889. Inflatable tires, the invention of Irish surgeon John Boyd Dunlop (1840–1921), gave a much softer ride.

Setting the style

It was the special combination of improvements—and the fact that he introduced them when there was a bicycling craze—that made the Rover a winning formula. Other manufacturers copied Starley's design, and the shape of the bicycle hardly changed for one hundred years.

Though engineers made every part of the bicycle lighter and better, Starley's basic design changed little until the 1990s. Then new—and immensely strong—carbon fiber materials made "one-piece" molded frames and wheels possible, as on this racing bicycle.

With a bigger front wheel, "high wheelers" in 1868 (below) went farther—and faster—with every turn of the pedals.

Safety bicycles, such as the Rover, (above) had a lower, less dangerous, riding position than the high wheelers that came before them. A chain powered the rear wheel.

VIDEO GAMES

The creators of the first video game did not devise it after a eureka moment. Nor did they do it for entertainment. Their aim in 1962 was to show off a brand-new computer—the size of a coat closet!

Simple beginnings

On a flickering, circular screen a triangle and a pencil shape chase each other around a glowing blob. If you squint your eyes, you can almost imagine that they are enemy spacecraft orbiting a distant planet. It is very different from the slick, lifelike graphics of a modern computer console, yet in 1962 this basic, jerky game—called *Space War*— amazed everyone who played it. This was the first time that anyone had seen an interactive computer with a video screen. Other computers at the time slowly printed out the results of programs on a roll of paper, so games as we play them today were impossible.

In *Space War* to move their "spaceships" on the round screen and to fire missiles players jiggled switches on the computer's cabinet. Like today's space games, rockets had limited fuel and weapons, as well as hyperspace, so they could disappear and reappear elsewhere.

Modern computer games look much more slick than *Space War*, but the challenges are the same. Players need similar skills, even if the target is a lifelike monster rather than a glowing triangle.

The DEC PDP-1 cost $120,000 in 1960, a time when construction workers earned around $1 per hour. It was stored in a huge cabinet and controlled by strips of paper tape punched with holes. The circular screen was the radical new feature that made the game possible.

Programming a legend

SpaceWar was the creation of Stephen Russell (1937–) and several of his friends at the Massachusetts Institute of Technology (MIT). They created the game to demonstrate an amazing new computer, the PDP-1. Russell wrote the main program in just a few months. His friends added details, including a "death star" with lifelike gravity and a realistic background of stars.

SpaceWar was so impressive that the manufacturer, DEC, built it into every computer that they sold. And despite the game's simplicity, it set the standard for an entertainment industry that is now bigger than movies.

SpaceWar was slow and clumsy, partly because the computer it ran on was designed to do many other types of work. Modern consoles, like this PlayStation, can create realistic, fast-changing images, not just because they are quicker but also because they are built specifically for video games.

THE WALKMAN

Music on the move was just a dream until the launch of the Walkman in 1979. We may think of these tiny tape players as a novel invention, and yet they contained no genuinely new technology. No flash of genius led to their creation. The idea came from a businessman who wanted to relieve the boredom of long airline flights.

But who was Masura Ibuka?

The man who inspired the Sony Walkman was born in Tokyo, Japan, (1908–1997). He studied engineering at college before founding the company that would later become Sony in 1946. With his partner, Akio Morita (1921–1999), he pioneered the tape recorders, televisions, and miniature radios that made the Sony label famous worldwide.

One good idea and a team of inventors

As the head of Sony Ibuka spent a lot of time flying between meetings on distant continents. To make the trips less tedious he asked Sony engineers in February 1979 if they could create a pocket-sized tape player so he could listen to high-quality stereo music without disturbing other passengers. The company's tape recorder division took only four days to build a prototype.

Before the Walkman was launched Sony executives feared that the lack of a loudspeaker would put off buyers. At the time headphones were big and heavy, and many Japanese people thought only the deaf wore them. So engineers developed special headphones (left) that were so small and light that music fans would hardly know they were wearing them.

The Sony Walkman was only a little bigger than the tapes it played—most other tape players were several times larger. Sony engineers kept the size down by printing the copper connections for electronic components on both sides of the machine's circuit boards. This was a daring new idea in 1979, but today every manufacturer does it.

The creation of the Walkman

Sony already sold journalists' miniature tape recorders, so they removed the recording mechanism and added circuits that would make them work in stereo. The high-quality music they played delighted Masura Ibuka and Akio Morita, Sony's head of marketing. Morita was so enthusiastic that he asked the engineers to have the machines ready to sell by the start of the summer vacation, less than four months away. He also wanted the players to be cheap enough for students to buy. This dismayed the engineers. To cut the price so low, they told their boss, they would have to make 30,000 tape players— twice the monthly sales of Sony's most popular model.

A success story

The engineers raced to build the new players by the summer deadline. The new tape player— called Walkman—was launched in June 1979 by fashion models on rollerblades, skateboards, and bicycles. There had not been time for market testing to see if the public would like the design, and for one anxious month dealers hardly sold any of the players. But then as word spread customers began buying them faster than Sony could make them. The Walkman turned out to be the company's biggest success story: by 1998 Sony had sold almost 250 million.

Sony engineers built Japan's first tape recorders in 1954, and the following year they launched the first pocket-sized transistor radios. Like the Walkman, their size helped make them successful.

THE INTERNET

The Internet began in the 1960s as a way to link many computers in different departments of the same company. But it only became a popular success from 1976, when two programmers found a way to make it appealing and easy for everyone to use.

But who is Tim Berners Lee?

British programmer Tim Berners Lee (1955–) built his first computer while studying at Oxford University in England. He worked as a software engineer at different companies before working at CERN.

And who is Mark Andreessen?

While in high school American Mark Andreessen (1971–) taught himself to program computers and tried to write a program that would do his math homework. As a college student he worked at the National Center for Supercomputing Applications, where he wrote Mosaic.

The Internet was created at the European Organization for Nuclear Research (CERN from the initials of its French name). Scientists there study the structure of atoms—tiny particles from which everything is made.

The birth of the Internet

Computers at CERN were linked by the Internet. But the information Tim Berners Lee used was scattered around many of them. So in 1976 he wrote a program to bring it all together on one single computer screen—his screen. He called the program "Enquire Within Upon Everything" after a famous old reference book. The program used hypertext—highlighted phrases that he clicked on to jump to new "pages" of information. In 1989 Lee realized that his idea could make it easy for anyone to use the Internet. With other CERN workers he devised a standard way of storing information and a new language —hypertext markup language, or HTML—for writing the pages that displayed it. They named the system the World Wide Web.

The Internet grew out of ARPANET, a group of linked computers that protected the United States against nuclear missiles. Scientists began using the system in the 1970s, and today the Internet links millions of computers.

Mosaic

Lee's program worked only on computers that scientists used until he made the code (program instructions) public. In the U.S. Mark Andreessen changed it to run on ordinary personal computers (PCs). He called it Mosaic. It was this "browser" that changed a little-known network of computers into a global way of exchanging information. The growth of the Internet was amazing. In 1993 there were only 50 servers (computers supplying Internet pages); the following year there were 10,000. Today there are almost 35 million.

Through the World Wide Web we can get pictures, sounds, and words from computers scattered all around the globe. We do not need to know where the information we want is stored—we just click to find it. Today this seems natural, but it was Lee's and Andreessen's work that made it all possible.

CHRONOLOGY OF INVENTORS

LIFE SPAN	INVENTOR	COUNTRY	INVENTION(S) AND PAGE NUMBER(S)
*287–212 B.C.	Archimedes	Greece	Principle of buoyancy, water-lifting screw 8
1564–1642	Galileo Galilei	Italy	Pendulum, motion of falling objects, motion of the planets 12
*born 1570	Hans Lippershey	Netherlands	Telescope 54
1642–1727	Isaac Newton	England	Theory of gravity, differential calculus, laws of motion, reflecting telescope 14, 55
1706–1790	Benjamin Franklin	U.S.	Lightning conductor, bifocals 62
1737–1798	Luigi Galvani	Italy	Battery 64
1740–1810	Joseph Montgolfier	France	Hot-air balloon 42
1745–1799	Jacques Montgolfier	France	Hot-air balloon 42
1745–1827	Alessandro Volta	Italy	Battery 64
1749–1823	Edward Jenner	Great Britain	Vaccination 18
1765–1825	Eli Whitney	U.S.	Cotton gin, interchangeable parts 16
1765–1833	Nicéphore Niepce	France	Photography 56
1787–1851	Louis Daguerre	France	Photography 56
1803–1865	Joseph Paxton	Great Britain	Ready-made buildings 20
1808–1896	Antonio Meucci	Italy/U.S.	Telephone 66
1811–1861	Elisha Otis	U.S.	Safety elevator 44
1837–1919	Richard Smith	Great Britain/Australia	Stump-jump plow 46
1839–1902	Almon Strowger	U.S.	Automatic telephone exchange 70
1843–1929	Elijah McCoy	U.S.	Automatic engine lubricator 78
1847–1931	Thomas Edison	U.S.	Electric lightbulb, sound recording, vacuum tube 68, 80
1851–1929	Emile Berliner	Germany/U.S.	Sound recording on disks, microphone 81
1854–1901	John Kemp Starley	Great Britain	Safety bicycle 82

1860–1951	Will Keith Kellogg	U.S.	Corn Flakes 22
1867–1912	Wilbur Wright	U.S.	Powered flight 48
1869–1942	Valdemar Poulsen	Denmark	Magnetic sound recording 81
1871–1948	Orville Wright	U.S.	Powered flight 48
1871–1955	Hubert Cecil Booth	Great Britain	Vacuum cleaner 24
1874–1937	Guglielmo Marconi	Italy	Radio communication 72
1881–1955	Alexander Fleming	Great Britain	Penicillium 28
1886–1956	Clarence Birdseye	U.S.	Frozen food 26
1888–1946	John Logie Baird	Great Britain	Television 74
1894–1970	Percy Lebaron Spencer	U.S.	Microwave oven 34
1896–1937	Wallace Carothers	U.S.	Nylon 30
1898–1968	Howard Florey	Australia	Penicillin 28
1904–1996	Julian Hill	U.S.	Nylon 30
1906–1979	Ernst Chain	Germany/Great Britain	Penicillin 28
1908–1997	Masura Ibuka	Japan	Walkman 86
1909–1991	Edwin Land	U.S.	Instant photography, Polaroid sunglasses and filters 58
1910–1994	Roy Plunkett	U.S.	Teflon 32
1910–1999	Christopher Cockerell	Great Britain	Hovercraft 50
1921–1999	Akio Morita	Japan	Walkman 86
born 1937	Stephen Russell	U.S.	Video games 84
born 1949	Paul Nurse	Great Britain	Sequencing the cancer gene 38
born 1950	Alec Jeffreys	Great Britain	DNA fingerprinting 36
born 1955	Tim Berners Lee	Great Britain	Internet 88
born 1971	Mark Andreessen	U.S.	World Wide Web browser 88

* approximate life span

GLOSSARY

AMBER
A rare type of hardened tree resin that looks like clear yellow plastic.

ANTISEPTIC
The ability to stop infections—or something that has this property.

ATMOSPHERE
The layer of gases, including life-giving oxygen, that surrounds our planet.

ATOMS
The tiny particles from which all matter—solid, liquid, or gas—is made.

BACTERIA
Minute creatures, visible only with a microscope, some of which cause diseases in plants and animals.

BROWSER
A program that enables a computer user to explore the Internet and view linked words, pictures, sounds, and movies.

CARPET BEATER
A cane or wire paddle that was once used to beat dirt out of carpets and rugs.

CIRCUIT BOARD
The plastic panel at the heart of most electronic devices. Copper wires printed on the board connect the electronic components attached to it.

COGWHEEL
A wheel with cogs (serrated teeth) around its edge that enable the wheel to function with another wheel so that both turn together.

COWPOX
A mild skin disease of cattle that is sometimes caught by people who care for the animals.

ELECTROMAGNET
A coil of wire that becomes magnetic when electricity flows through it.

EUREKA MOMENT
A sudden brilliant idea that leads to a new discovery or invention.

FILAMENT
A threadlike part of an object, such as the thin wire inside an electric lightbulb, that glows white-hot when electricity flows through it.

GEAR
A cogwheel or a collection of cogwheels linked together.

GENERATOR
A machine that produces electric power when operated.

GENES
Small parts of DNA, the long molecule that contains the "design" for all living things. Passed on from parents to their children, individual genes carry the code for features such as hair and eye color.

GREENHOUSE
A glass-walled building that uses the sun's heat to help plants grow more quickly.

IMMUNE
Protected against infection by a particular disease.

IODINE
A dark gray crystal that is antiseptic in small quantities but poisonous in large doses. Iodine combines with silver metal to make a chemical that darkens in the daylight.

IRON OXIDE
A chemical with the common name "rust" that forms when oxygen in the air reacts with wet iron and steel.

MAGNETRON
An electronic device used to produce microwave energy in an oven or radar device.

MASS
How much material an object contains—the greater an object's mass, the stronger gravity's pull is on it and thus the greater its weight.

MERCURY
A poisonous silver metal that is liquid at room temperature.

MIGRAINE
A severe, pounding headache that often causes nausea and blurred vision.

MORSE CODE
A series of long and short bursts of electricity, sound, or light used to carry messages.

MOLD
A type of tiny fungus that forms a furlike coating on rotting animal or plant material.

NOBEL PRIZE
A valuable prize awarded each year to the best individual in physics, chemistry, medicine, literature, economics, and peace.

PATENT
A special type of protection for an invention that makes it public knowledge but stops anyone from copying it until the inventor has had the chance to profit from it.

PLASTIC
A material, usually made from oil, that can be easily molded and shaped.

POLYMER
A type of plastic created by making many small molecules of a gas or liquid join together to form a long chain with very different properties.

PULSE
The throbbing beat that can be felt on the body of a living human or animal as the heart pumps blood.

RADIATION
Any of a series of waves, including light, microwaves, radio, and radar; but most often used to mean powerful waves, like X rays, that can harm living material.

RADIO WAVE
Form of radiation commonly used to broadcast messages and entertainment.

RIB
Thin, curved chest bone—or an object that resembles such a bone.

SANATORIUM
A resort or treatment center for those who are sick or who imagine they are.

SILK
The fine thread produced by silkworms or the valuable fabric woven from such threads.

SILKWORM
The caterpillar of an Asian moth, bred and raised for the silk it spins.

SLAVERY
A system in which captive people are bought and sold as possessions and forced to work, often without pay and without the rights that free people enjoy.

SLOGAN
A short, snappy, easily remembered phrase used to advertise a product.

SMALLPOX
A dangerous, easily spread disease that kills many of those it infects and leaves survivors' skin marked by scars.

SPOKES
Thick, straight wires joining the rim of a wheel to the central hub around which it spins.

TECHNOLOGY
Applying science in a useful way.

TRANSMITTER
An instrument that sends out a communication signal.

TUMOR
An uncontrolled growth of cells, such as cancer, that sometimes leads to sickness or death.

UNDERTAKER
Someone whose job it is to prepare the dead for burial or cremation (burning).

VACCINE
A deliberately weakened form of a disease that, when injected or swallowed, provides immunity from infection.

VAPOR
A gaslike form of a substance that is usually liquid or solid.

VEGETARIAN
Someone who eats no meat or who eats only vegetables.

YEAST
A simple, microscopic plant valued for its ability to turn sugar into alcohol and carbon dioxide gas.

INDEX

ACKNOWLEDGMENTS

The publisher would like to thank the following for permission to reproduce their material. Every care has been taken to trace copyright holders. However, if there have been unintentional omissions or failure to trace copyright holders, we apologize and will, if informed, endeavor to make corrections in any future edition.

Key: B = bottom, C = center, L = left, R = right, T = top

5TR Cancer Research (U.K.); 8TC Popperfoto; 9CC Bettmann/Corbis; 9TC Bettmann/Corbis; 9RC Sony Corporation; 12CL Science Museum/Science & Society library; 12TR Science Museum/Science & Society Library; 13BR Digitalvision Limit; 14BL Getty Images/World Perspectives; 14TR Crown Copyright/Brogdale Horticultural Trust; 15BLC Courtesy of Chip Simon; 16CLC Bettmann/Corbis; 16BC Bettmann/Corbis; 17BLC Richard Hamilton Smith/Corbis; 18TRC Hulton-Deutsch Collection/Corbis; 18BLC Bettmann/Corbis; 19TR BSIP, Villareal/Science Photo Library;19BL Roger Harris/Science Photo Library; 20–21B Courtesy of Richard Platt; 20CL Science Museum, London/Heritage-Images; 20TC Courtesy of Richard Platt; 21CRC Paul Almasy/Corbis; 22BR The Advertising Archive; 24TR Getty Images; 24BL Science Museum/Science & Society Picture Library; 25TR Science Museum/Science & Society Picture Library; 25BC Dyson Graphics; 27B Rosenfeld Images Ltd/Science Photo Library; 27TR BSIP Bernard/Science Photo Library; 27C Electric Corp./National Geographic Image Collection; 28CL Hulton-Deutsch Collection/Corbis; 28C Science Photo Library; 28TRC Science Pictures Limited/Corbis; 28BRC Bettmann/Corbis; 30TR Courtesy of DuPont; 31BL Courtesy of DuPont; 31TRC Hulton-Deutsch Collection/Corbis; 32C Dr. Jeremy Burgess/Science Photo Library; 32CL Courtesy of DuPont; 32B NASA/Science Photo Library; 33TR Courtesy of the Hagley Museum and Library; 34TL Raytheon Company Photo; 34BC © Bettmann/Corbis; 35BC Raytheon Company Photo; 36CL David Parker/Science Photo Library; 36TR J. C. Revy/Science Photo Library; 37C Tek Image/Science Photo Library; 37BRC Corbis Sygma; 38B Dr Gopal Murti/Science Photo Library; 39TL Alfred Pasieka/Science Photo Library; 39CR Philippe Plailly/Eurelios/Science Photo Library; 39BC Roger Ressmeyer/Corbis; 42TC © Duomo/Corbis; 42CL Mary Evans Picture Library; 42CB Mary Evans Picture Library; 42C Sheila Terry/Science Photo Library; 42–43C © Royalty-free/Corbis; 43TC, TR, CR Vince Streano/Corbis; 43BC Popperfoto; 43TRC Corbis; 44CLC Bettmann/Corbis; 44–45C Science Photo Library; 45TRC David Lees/Corbis; 46TR Courtesy of Mortlock Library of South Australia; 47BRC Beryl E. Neumann, for the National Trust of Australia/The Smith Brothers and the Stump-Jump Plow; 47TRC Beryl E. Neumann, for the National Trust of Australia/The Smith Brothers and the Stump Jump Plough; 48–49BC Bettmann/Corbis; 48CLC Bettmann/Corbis; 50BLC Hulton-Deutsch Collection/Corbis; 50TRC Hovercraft Museum Trust; 51BRC Bettmann/Corbis; 51C © Hovercraft Museum Trust; 54CLC Bettmann/Corbis; 54TR Science Photo Library; 55BLC Roger Ressmeyer/Corbis; 55CRC Roger Ressmeyer/Corbis; 56TR Science Museum/Science & Society Photo Library; 56CL Mary Evans Picture Library; 56–57BC Harry Ransom Humanities Research Center, The University of Texas at Austin; 57TR Courtesy of Richard Platt; 57C Science Museum/Science & Society Photo Library/Daguerre; 58BL Robert Harding Picture Library/U.S.—Boston, Massachusetts, The Polaroid Factory; 58TR Science Museum/Science & Society Photo Library; 59CL Popperfoto; 59BR Polaroid Corporation; 59TR National Museum of Photography, Film & TV/Science & Society Picture Library; 62CR Mary Evans Picture Library; 62CL Library of Congress/Science Photo Library; 62BL Science Museum/Science & Society Photo Library; 63TR Jean-Loup Charmet/Science Photo Library; 64BL Courtesy of Richard Platt; 64TR Courtesy of Richard Platt; 65TR Mary Evans Picture Library; 66CL (head only) Science Photo Library; 67TR Courtesy Garibaldi-Meucci Museum, Staten Island, N.Y.; 66–67BL, BR Mary Evans Picture Library; 66TR J-L Charmet/Science Photo Library; 67 (head only) Mary Evans Picture Library; 68CL Science Museum/Science & Society Photo Library; 68TR Science Museum/Science & Society Photo Library; 69CR From the collections of Henry Ford Museum & Greenfield Village; 70BL, 71 BR Science Photo Library; 70–71B Courtesy of Richard Platt; 71TR Science Museum/Science & Society Photo Library; 72C Nik Wheeler/Corbis; 72BR Bettmann/Corbis; 73BR D. Roberts/Science Photo Library; 73TC Bettmann/Corbis; 74BLC Bettmann/Corbis; 74BLC Bettmann/Corbis; 74TR Science Museum/Science & Society Picture Library; 75TR Mary Evans Picture Library; 75BL Musee de Radio-France, Paris, France/Bridgeman Art Library; 78CL Courtesy of State Archives of Michigan; 78C From the collections of Henry Ford Museum & Greenfield Village Research Center; 78–79 Minnesota Historical Society/Corbis; 80BL Science Museum, London, U.K./Bridgeman Art Library; 80TR Corbis; 80BR Science Museum/Science & Society Picture Library; 81TRC Hulton-Deutsch Collection/Corbis; 81BL Science Museum/Science & Society Picture Library; 81BC Science Museum/Science & Society Picture Library; 81BR Science Museum/Science & Society Picture Library; 82TR Mary Evans Picture Library; 83CR Mary Evans Picture Library; 85BR Sony Computer Entertainment Europe/Sony Playstation®; 85TRC 2000 by Maury Markowitz, www.sympatico.ca; 86CL Sony Corporation; 86C © James A. Sugar/Corbis; 87BRC Bettmann/Corbis; 88C www.geocities.com/Heartland/valley.htm; 88C Henry Horenstein/Corbis; 88BLC © Telehouse; 88TR Charles E. Rotkin/Corbis

The publisher would like to thank the following illustrators:
Mark Bristow 2–3, 12–13C, 21TR, 29BL, 30C, 44BL, 44–45C, 46BL, 54BR, 55TR, 62–63C, 82–83BC, 87TR, 86–87C; Mike Buckley 36–37C; Tom Connell 14–15R, 22–23C, 34–35TL; Richard Platt 17TR, 46BR, 48TR; Jurgen Ziewe 8–9C, 26BL, 64–65C, 68–69C, 84–85C

The author, Richard Platt, would like to thank the following for their assistance:
John Gustafson; Norman Krim, Raytheon archivist; Lori Lohmeyer, Nation's Restaurant News; Paul Stevenson, Stockton Reference Library; Ross Macmillan and Hugh Turral, Agricultural Engineering, University of Melbourne; Marilyn Ward, Royal Agricultural and Horticultural Society of South Australia